UNDERSTANDING THE
I CHING

UNDERSTANDING THE I CHING

The history and use of the world's most ancient system of divination

by

Tom Riseman

The Aquarian Press
An Imprint of HarperCollins*Publishers*

The Aquarian Press
An Imprint of HarperCollins*Publishers*
77–85 Fulham Palace Road,
Hammersmith, London W6 8JB

This edition 1990
First published by The Aquarian Press
as Introduction to the I Ching 1980
3 5 7 9 10 8 6 4 2

Tom Riseman asserts the moral right to
be identified as the author of this work

A CIP catalogue record for this book
is available from the British Library

ISBN 0-85030-985-9

Printed in Great Britain by
HarperCollinsManufacturing, Glasgow

CONTENTS

INTRODUCTION

Among the *I Ching's* many virtues is one singularly important to us in the West — namely, its ability to suggest with increasing clarity levels of reality diametrically opposed to our own. The quaint and often bizarre language of the *I Ching* seems to bear little relation to our everyday world, but its naturalistic, intuitive approach and its extraordinary perceptions are complementary to our deductive 'logical' thinking.

The *I Ching* states that change is a constant, enduring force that is everywhere and in everything. Whoever understands that force, and its state of development, at a certain time, truly knows the situation. Obscure as this sounds, the successes of the *I Ching* are amply charted. C. G. Jung, the first psychologist to discover man's need for wholeness and order, had the *I Ching* firmly in mind when he coined the term 'Synchronicity' to describe the connections that appear between apparently unconnected events.

The relationship we form with the *I Ching* at first need not be based on understanding the system. It is enough that we establish contact with what Jung called the *I Ching's* 'unique psychology'. Since their origin and style are of ancient China, the hexagrams and the traditional commentaries are flowery and abstruse; but they describe fundamental, root causes which are as relevant to the urban neurotic as they were to the Chinese scholar. The only limitations on using the *Book of Changes* lie in our minds.

The highest goal of the *I Ching*, like all ontological systems is self-knowledge. The *I Ching* is not for the frivolous or weak-minded; but with a little determination and sense it can become a powerful source of wisdom, inspiration and knowledge for anyone who respects its methods and its principles.

Origins and History of the I Ching

Few works have had an unbroken history as long and distinguised as the *I Ching*. The legendary sage Fu Hsi is credited with the discovery of the eight basic trigrams — although their names are probably not even Chinese, which puts their origin somewhat vaguely between 25,000 and 5,000 years ago.

Two arrangements of the trigrams were in use by 1150 BC, when the imprisonment of King Wen by a jealous emperor provided him with eleven years in which to produce an expanded and philosophically broader version of the *I Ching*. This he did by combining the eight trigrams into 64 six-line hexagrams and adding commentaries ('Judgements') to each one. He also commented extensively on the logic and mystical philosophy behind the hexagrams and his work forms the most important part of the Ten Wings — the most erudite commentary on the *I Ching* that has evolved over the ages.

Wen's son, Tan, added further hexagram commentaries, but it was Confucius who made the profundities of these authors accessible to ordinary scholars during the fifth century. It was he who first named the *I Ching* 'The Changes' and he produced study after study of it.

INTRODUCTION

Taoism

Taoism is inseparable from the philosophy of the *I Ching*. It is based on the complementary yet antagonistic principles of yin and yang, both creating and destroying each other by the ceaseless rearrangements of their relationship. The basic rule they obey is life's only certainty — that of change. The *I Ching*, too, takes eternal change as its basis, arranging each of the 64 hexagrams into six lines that change from yin to yang, or vice versa, thus, step by step, changing the hexagram into a completely different state. In this way a force, depicted in its abstract form within the Judgements and Images, can be seen building up from infancy to climax and point of decay in every hexagram.

Ancient and Modern Uses

When China formed the world's first civil service, the *I Ching* provided a philosophical framework for governmental and everyday matters. In everything, the oracle was consulted, the fortune-tellers moving from market to market to cast their yarrow stalks over small portable tables.

In modern times Chian Kai-Shek extolled the *I Ching* as an oracle and a basis of the 'Ultimate Virtues' of the Chinese. Use of the *I Ching* was widespread throughout the East during the Second World War. As the leading classic on tactics, it was almost *de rigeur* for staff-level officers in the armed forces, and there is still a widely-held view among Japanese intellectuals that the Imperial Navy would have won the Pacific campaign if so many aggressive naval officers had not considered themselves too 'modern' to consult the oracle.

No such conceit afflicted Mao Tse-Tung, who consulted the book regularly during the years of planning and fighting that led to the Long March. It is still widely used in the East, although many now prefer simplified versions.

The *I Ching* is now taking its place throughout the world alongside astrology, palmistry and other 'occult' arts as a businessman's tool. One large computer company has already started a programme of intensive research into numerological systems, which stem from the framework of the *I Ching*. A small, battery-powered, silicon chip '*I Ching* Computer', which performs the coin-throwing or yarrow-casting function, has been available for some time in America, where it is widely used in stock market commodities dealing.

Motives and Attitudes

Questioning and interpreting the oracle requires both precision and an open mind. Often this means suspending disbelief as far as possible to allow the subtle and frequently confusing images to penetrate the mind.

No psychic talents are necessary, but one's attitude is of fundamental importance. If the oracle is treated like a party game it will give party game answers. The first step is to be respectful, which is why a ritual formality can be helpful.

There are two main methods: yarrow stalks or coins. The latter requires three old Chinese coins, which are round with square central holes. Modern equivalents for both can be used — copper coins or plain sticks about eight inches in length. The coins should be washed thoroughly before first use and then held between the palms for ten minutes or so and never lent to others.

Any sort of question can be asked, but selfishness will 'corrupt' or cloud the response. Answers will be clearest if the questions require a set of circumstances to be described and have a time factor included. Thus, questions requiring a simple 'Yes' or 'No' answer may receive apparently obscure responses. Address the oracle, silently or aloud, with your clearly-framed question. Treat the oracle as if it were a much-respected person. Then cast the oracle while retaining the question in your mind.

Casting With Coins

The coins may be held and then thrown lightly onto a flat surface. Do not begin, however, until the question is quite clear in your mind: a cloudy question will produce a cloudy answer. The side of the coin with four figures (Chinese coins) is considered yang, like the heads side of modern coins, and is given the value three. The reverse is given the value two. The coins are tossed six times: each time, a total value of six, seven, eight or nine will be produced.

Write down the total after each throw, or throw the hexagram immediately. It starts from the bottom, since all organic life grows upwards. A six equals Old Yin; seven means Young Yang; eight is Young Yin; nine, Old Yang. You can use a single horizontal line for yang and a broken line for yin. In addition, mark these with a central circle or cross to represent Old Yang and Old Yin respectively. (Alternatively, represent a six with a cross, a seven with a dot, an eight with two dots, and a nine with a circle.)

The significance of the 'Old' lies in the fundamental philosophy of the T'ai Chi, which states that when a force reaches a climax, or becomes 'old', it changes to its opposite: thus, the 'Old' lines are 'changing' and they may occur at any one, or several, points in the six lines, emphasizing the particular condition described there. One might, for instance, throw six, seven, eight, eight, seven, eight. These would be: Old Yin, Young Yang, Young Yin, Young Yin, Young Yang and Young Yin respectively.

Referring to the tables (Appendix), which list the eight trigrams, we cross-refer the lower and upper trigram and get hexagram 29, K'an, with a changing line in the first place. We then read the Judgement and the Image, plus the commentary on the line, and then turn to the new hexagram produced by the change of the first line. This is now yang, so the resulting hexagram will be Chieh, number 60 — the eventual outcome of your situation.

11

Interpretation

There are three major factors in judging an answer:

1. Each hexagram represents a unique, complex type of energy, like a musical note formed by thousands of harmonies. It is important to remember that what is pictured may often be the factors underlying one's situation rather than a literal picture of the situation itself.

2. Each hexagram and each line can represent, broadly, three things: i) a set of circumstances, ii) one's own situation, iii) the relationship between oneself and others.

3. Human situations have many complex factors underlying them. Your understanding of the answer will depend upon your degree of involvement with the subject. Thus, it is important to be aware of your position in relation to the situation and to the oracle. In this way you can judge at what level you are asking a question and how to interpret the answer.

THE HEXAGRAMS

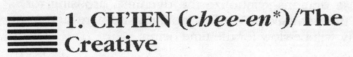

1. CH'IEN (*chee-en**)/The Creative

Upper and lower trigrams are both Ch'ien; all lines unbroken and represent yang — strong, active, giving, spiritually and mentally orientated and consistent.

Ch'ien has the attributes of heaven, the king, the leader and the family head. It represents someone who uses his power and vitality constructively. Primal energy becomes its opposite after reaching its climax. Thus the hexagrams warns of success turning to failure if strength is excessive or arrogant.

The Judgement

The Creative brings sublime success,
Benefiting all with perseverence.

The earliest meaning of Ch'ien was a 'force of success'

---

* The older, Wade-Giles system of romanization is more suited to the ancient names than the official Chinese system, Pinyin. So the old style has been used, followed by as precise a phonetic rendering as possible.

flowing from the depths. But everything depends on the individual persevering in the correct way — that is, doing what is right.

The Image

Heaven's movement is full of power.
So does the superior man strengthen himself.
Heaven moves unceasingly. This should be an example. Make the self strong, effective and enduring.

The Lines

Nine at the bottom: the dragon hibernates.
Do not act.
Chinese dragons symbolize the dynamic, arousing force. Your time will come — but not yet. Prepare and wait. Activity will be slow for the time being.

Nine in the second place: the dragon appears on the field.
Benefit in seeing the great one.
You should gain some improvement in your situation and your efforts will be appreciated. Seek advice or help from your elders or betters if you can.

Nine in the third place: the superior man is actively creative throughout the day.
He ponders the evening long.
Danger. No blame.
There is much to be done, without great reward. Beware of pitfalls and remain correct: in difficult circumstances.

Nine in the fourth place: the dragon hovers over the deep.
No blame.
It is a time of choice. To strike upwards, or withdraw? There is no 'right' and no 'wrong' way: the guidelines are within oneself.

Nine in the fifth place: dragon in the heavens.

Benefit in seeing the great one.

An influential person may recognize your talent and help you. Your influence will spread and you will meet people of like kind. Paradoxically, you may be in a lonely position as well.

Nine in the sixth place: the dragon is arrogant.
Cause for repentance

Material or mental isolation will lead to a fall if you continue in this way.

▤ 2. K'UN (*kw'n*)/The Receptive

Each line represents the dark, earth, mother force, yin, with the attribute of devotion. This is not weakness, but a primary force, like Chi'ien. these first two are not, however, opposites. They represent the king and the queen, or the father and the mother. Only when the Yielding is led by the Creative can a constructive result emerge.

The Judgement

The Receptive brings great success and benefits through the
  quality of a mare.
The superior man leads an undertaking and goes astray:
Later he receives guidance.
Find friends in the south and west: forego them in the
  north and east.
Peaceful perseverance. Good fortune.

The mare-like quality (perseverance) of the Receptive is quite different from the active persistence of Chi'en and indicates more material circumstances. Be guided and supporting.

South and west symbolizes effort and work. Thus, north and east, or commands and planning with others, should be rejected in favour of solitude.

The Image

The earth's condition is devotion.
Thus the superior man, with great character, bears the world.

The earth sustains everything, good and evil. The superior man is pure, broad, and deep in character, so he can accept and support his situation.

The Lines

Six at the bottom: hoarfrost underfoot, solid ice will follow.
The signs of dark and cold increase. Misfortune is building up.

Six in the second place: straight, square, great.
No artifice, everything benefits.

The Receptive (symbolized by a square) yields to the yang (straight) force, producing good results in a natural way. Things turn out well.

Six in the third place: hidden ability remains and perseveres.
Serving the king, bring quietly to completion.

Hide your light. quiet effort will bring rewards, so develop projects which will bear fruit later.

Six in the fourth place: the sack is tied.
No praise, no blame.

Be reserved: act with great caution if things go wrong.

Six in the fifth place: a plain yellow lower garment means supreme good fortune.

Yellow means reliability: aristocrats (the most reserved in behaviour) wore plain clothes below the waist. A time of achievement — but indirectly, and through discretion, especially in public.

Six at the top: dragons fight in the field.
Black and yellow blood.

The changing line symbolizes the two primal forces struggling for the place which should be that of heaven (black, or dark blue). Beware of quarrels — two sides are in opposition, and both may be hurt.

☵☳ 3. CHUN (*Jw'n*)/Difficulty in the Beginning

K'an above and Chen below bring clouds, water, movement and thunder together. Thus, a time of tension.

Chun is the time when sprouts struggle to push through the hard ground with great difficulty.
One should be very patient.

The Judgement

Difficulty in the Beginning means great success and benefit through perseverence.
Nothing should be begun; helpers should be found.
Everything is unformed and struggling. If one perseveres, a great success may follow. However, precipitate or premature action will bring disaster.

The Image

Clouds and thunder: Difficulty at the Beginning.
The superior man makes order from chaos.
Storm-clouds have definite form: One should sort out what is what and be ready to take advantage of better conditions after the rain.

The Lines

Nine at the bottom: difficulty and consideration.
Benefit if one perseveres correctly.
Do not hesitate, but do not hurry or force the pace. Simply

17

persevere and maintain humility, especially if you find helpers.

> *Six in the second place: things are split apart by a*
> * horseman.*
> *He is not a robber: he wishes to woo.*
> *But the girl is demure.*
> *Ten years, then she accepts and commits.*

Sudden changes of affairs, perhaps a shock. Change to a high-powered approach. Avoid the helping hand which brings obligation. Success only after the completion of the current cycle of difficulties.

> *Six in the third place: one hunting deer without the guide*
> * can only lose his way in the forest.*
> *The superior man understands this, and prefers to turn*
> * back.*
> *Continuing brings regret.*

Premature action, without the correct authority or guidance, brings deep disgrace. One may be held back by a person in trouble. Do not force issues.

> *Six in the fourth place: a horse and cart are parted.*
> *Seek union and take the step.*
> *Everything brings benefit.*

An unusual opportunity should be taken. The first step may involve embarrassment, but recognition will come.

> *Nine in the fifth place: difficulty in good works.*
> *Good fortune for small things; great things find*
> * misfortune.*

Carry on, step by step, being correct and expecting no great success.

> *Six at the top: horse and cart are parted and blood mixes*
> * with tears.*

A sudden twist in events, combined with arrogance, can bring great misfortune, or make us give up. One should immediately change one's attitudes.

☶ 4. MENG (*m'ng*)/Youth

The hexagram implies immaturity and purity. The upper trigram, Ken, means the youngest child or mountain; K'an, beneath, means danger or water. Hence the images of a spring gushing at the mountain's foot, and a foolish child. Youth requires instruction and, overall, this hexagram implies teaching and, in particular, being patient and consistently forebearing.

The Judgement

Youthful folly succeeds.
It is not I seeking the immature youth;
He seeks me.
I respond to his first questioning;
If he persists, it is disrespectful.
If he is disrespectful, I give him no answer.
Benefit in persevering.

A double idea is presented: the oracle and its attitude to its questioners, with the idea of people in learning situations. The immature questioner must learn to accept the relationship of master and pupil implied in using the I Ching.

Similarly, the advice on conduct is that a good student is repectful, hardworking, and masters each step as he goes.

The Image

A spring gushes beneath the mountain;
Symbolizing Youth.
The superior man develops himself
Through correct vigour.

Like the good student, one should cultivate one's character with clarity and perseverance.

The Lines

> *Six at the bottom: to train a youth, it is better to use discipline.*
> *Shackles should be removed, or humiliation follows.*

Imitation begins education. From then on, the youth must have a serious approach, or he will remain foolish and unappreciative. But meaningless, restricting routines cripple the mind. A time of entanglements and difficulty, which should work out.

> *Nine in the second place: treating folly kindly brings good fortune.*
> *Understanding this way with women brings good fortune.*
> *The son can take charge of the household.*

These lines picture a man with the strength of mind necessary to assist the weak, to maintain virtuous chivalry and build a personality fit for higher responsibility. This is a time of harmony and achievement.

> *Six in the third place: do not choose a maiden who, when a rich man comes near, loses her self-possession. No benefit.*

Do not throw yourself away. No value will result, and you will lose your dignity. Remain modest, quiet and correct.

> *Six in the fourth place: a youth in confusion finds humiliation.*

If you are involved with an unrealistic person, withdraw. You will be humiliated if you continue. People will think poorly of you.

> *Six in the fifth place: youthful innocence brings good fortune.*

Innocence is necessary — that is, lack of preconceptions, plus respect for one's teacher. Success in your aims.

> *Line at the top: in punishing youth, there is no benefit in oneself transgressing.*
> *The only benefit is preventing further mischief.*

Be cautious. You may be punished or be the one who punishes, but let the punishment fit the 'crime'.

 5. HSU (*shu*) /Contemplation (Nourishment)

The trigram K'an (water, danger) above Ch'ien (heaven, strength) indicates rain-clouds in the sky. It will rain, but meanwhile one must wait. Use the time in preparation. The idea is enlarged by that of contemplation, which originates in the ancient ideagram Hsu, representing a sitting medita- tor. Contemplation also contains the idea of (nourishing) the core of vital energy (*prana* or *ch'i*) in the tanden or centre of the body. You should proceed cautiously, but ambitiously. Beware of competition, but do not treat competitors harshly.

The Judgement

> *Contemplation. If sincere, you gain glory.*
> *Perseverance brings good fortune.*
> *Benefit in crossing the great water.*

Inner certainty, and recognition of things as they are is true 'sincerity'. This must be followed by resolute, consistent action and application. It is advantageous to travel, or take a major decision, or make great changes.

The Image

> *Clouds rise to heaven, symbolizing Contemplation.*
> *The superior man, eating and drinking, is content.*

Rain comes after clouds, but we can only wait. If we are wise, we nourish our bodies through proper eating and our minds through cultivating calm. Then we will be ready when the time comes and, in the meantime, be content.

The Lines

Nine at the bottom: waiting in the field.
Benefit from remaining in what is lasting. No regret.
A feeling of mild agitation and dissatisfaction. One feels events looming. Avoid precipitous action and lead a well-ordered life.

Nine in the second place: waiting on the shore inspires gossip.
Eventual good fortune.
Danger (water) is near and strife can easily develop. Remain calm and magnanimous and things will resolve themselves.

Nine in the third place: stuck in the mud, encourages the enemy.
You are in an exposed position. Be cautious in relationships and, guard against loss of possessions or status.

Six in the fourth place: waiting in blood.
Escape from the pit.
You are isolated and in an extremely dangerous situation. The only way out is to retain one's composure and wait. No chance of success now — one can only try to survive.

Nine in the fifth place: waiting at the meal.
Perseverance brings good fortune.
Things go well: enjoy your good fortune and maintain a calm and relaxed attitude. Continue your efforts towards a fixed goal, without haste.

Six at the top: falling into the abyss.
Three unexpected guests appear: treat them with courtesy.
Eventual good fortune.
All one's plans will be overturned and one must yield gracefully. There is a ray of hope after the disaster. Examine it well and use it wisely. Be cautious and alert and you will benefit.

6. SUNG (*soong*)/Conflict

The upward movement of Ch'ien (heaven) conflicts with
the downward flow of water (K'an, the bottom trigram). A
fundamental difference is expressed and enlarged by the
attributes of the trigrams — strength above cunning. The
upper trigram is also in front, so we have force in front of
cunning, suggesting a quarrelsome nature.

The Judgement

Conflict. You are sincere,
Despite being obstructed.
Halt halfway — good fortune;
Completing brings misfortune.
Benefit from seeing the great man,
Not in crossing the greater water.

Conflict develops through conviction — in other words,
egoism. Be clear-headed and fair enough to compromise or
give in. This applies especially if one is clinging stubbornly to
an uncertain viewpoint. Seek advice or arbitration from a
higher authority or wiser person. When energies are divided,
do not attempt undertakings which require concerted energies.

The Image

Heaven and water move in opposite directions,
Symbolizing Conflict.
Thus the superior man
Carefully considers the beginnings of all enterprises.

Conflict is latent. Only by profound and meticulous ordering
of aims, in advance, can it be prevented from emerging.

The Lines

Six at the bottom: even if one does not continue the affair,
There is gossip. Good fortune in the end.

Disputes and a malicious atmosphere are likely, but will clear up. Do not force things, and avoid confrontations.

Nine in the second place: one cannot continue this.
Retreating, he returns home.
The three hundred households of the town avoid tragedy.

One should not confront an enemy bigger than oneself, but retreat or make peace. Quiet-living people will do well; others may be forced into conflict.

Six in the third place: dependence on traditions brings danger.
Good fortune in the end.
If you serve the king, seek no fame.

Depend upon what you yourself have discovered or earned. Seek no praise or recognition. In general, there are no great successes or failures.

Nine in the fourth place: one cannot continue this.
Retreating, he resigns himself, and finds peace.
Good fortune.

You are wrong in your conflict and turning back brings peace. After a recent loss, the tide turns in your favour.

Nine in the fifth place: taking conflict to his judgement brings great good fortune.

Wise counsel or binding arbitration from a higher power is appropriate. One will gain recognition or promotion, if deserving.

Nine at the top: even if he is given a fine belt, it will be snatched away three times in a morning.

After apparent success over others comes unhappiness and more conflict. Nothing is settled. But those living quietly will find life easy.

▤ 7. SHIH (*shrr*)/The Army

The Army represents massed forces, with an objective in

view. Water (the lower trigram, K'an) trapped by earth (K'un, above) represents powerful forces held in check by a common discipline or by the direction of someone in authority.

The unbroken line represents the leader. However, because it occupies the lower trigram, he is not the head of the state. Therefore he must act correctly and in a trustworthy fashion. He must also have the respect of his men for the army to remain effective.

The Judgement

The Army. The army must have perseverance
And a strong leader.
Good fortune and no blame.

The situations requires a strong man. However, the one who should lead is at present not sufficiently involved with those around him. He must draw others to him by demonstrating the common needs, and his fitness to lead.

The Image

In the earth is water,
Symbolizing the Army.
The superior man increases his following
Through benevolence towards the masses.

Only by fair peacetime policies will a leader have support in war. Likewise, a sense of trust and common values are necessary between those seeking to mend their differences, or to engage in an undertaking together.

The Lines

Six at the bottom: an army should move according to its
   orders.
Ominous, if not so.

The time is right for new undertakings or forging ahead

with work. But underlying principles, motives and tactics must be good, or serious trouble will start. You may have already made a premature start.

> *Nine in the second place: the leader works amongst his men: the king thrice honours him.*
> *Good fortune without blame.*

A person of influence helps you towards your goal. You will receive promotion and recognition, and your success will be shared by associates.

> *Six in the third place: the army carries corpses in a cart.*
> *Ominous.*

Having over-estimated your virtues and overlooked your weaknesses, misfortune inevitably follows. Apparent success will be valueless.

> *Six in the fourth place: the army makes a strategic retreat.*
> *No blame.*

Avoid trouble by well-planned withdrawal. In no sense is this a final defeat.

> *Six in the fifth place: wildlife enters the fields.*
> *There is benefit in catching it and no blame.*
> *The eldest son should lead the army.*
> *The younger carries corpses.*
> *Continuing is ominous.*

The army does not have an effective leader, therefore enemy forces have broken into one's territory. Thus, vigorous and experienced leadership is required. Overall, your handling of the situation to date has been unequal to its demands. You cannot continue like this.

> *Six at the top: the generalissimo makes proclamations, founds states, awards manorial rights.*
> *Small men should not be given power.*

One breaks free of obstacles and life appears to take a turn for the better. But beware of your own complacency and unjust methods. Do not give rewards for old times' sake.

☵☷ 8. PI (*bee*)/Union

Above is K'an, water: below is K'un, earth. This natural mixture indicates a person or a time of co-operation and goodwill. It indicates good fortune in personal affairs and business, provided there is trust, commitment, and honesty.

The Judgement

Union: good fortune.
Enquire further of the oracle.
Is your spirit great, firm and persevering?
If so, make no mistakes.
He who hesitates may come too late.
Misfortune.

Every union requires a strong centre. A group forms its relationships in a definite, delicate manner, and late comers cannot share the same depth of union as earlier members. Accept the restraints of the union if you wish to receive its benefits — otherwise leave.

The Image

Water on the earth,
Symbolizing Union.
The kings of old established manorial boundaries,
Cultivating friendly relations with their barons.

Water is absorbed by the earth and they form a natural union. Thus, kings awarded lands to their nobles, assiduously working to ensure all understood the advantages of union.

The Lines

Six at the bottom: sincere, respectful union;
There can be no mistakes.
Inner truth, like a full bowl.
Good fortune accrues and manifests.

The fundamental, and only, basis for true relationships, is sincerity and real appreciation. This is not always obvious on the outside. Like a full bowl of food, what is inside is important. One may have help in work and friendships.

> *Six in the second place: instinctive union.*
> *Continuing brings good fortune.*

Dignity in responding freely to others. Expect unusual help, though formal relationships may be less than smooth.

> *Six in the third place: union with the wrong characters.*

Intimate relationships with unsuitable characters weaken and confuse one. Desist, or harm will result. If others in this association are not actually bad, one can remain sociable. One should note and beware of others' attitudes.

> *Six in the fourth place: union from without.*
> *Continuing brings good fortune.*

Your contact with someone at the centre of a union is already close. Do not hide your relationship. Stick to your principles.

> *Nine in the fifth place: most honourable union.*
> *The king's gamekeepers drive the game from three sides only.*
> *The people have no fear. Good fortune.*

Beaters at hunts left one escape route, so some beasts were captured whilst others turned away. One should not coerce anyone into union. In this way the relationship is natural and sincere. Difficulties at first, followed by smooth conditions if one acts correctly.

> *Six at the top: union without a leader. Ominous.*

If one vacillates and is both unable to commit oneself at the appropriate time and unable to withdraw, there can be no satisfaction for anyone involved. A time of difficulty.

☰ 9. HSIAO CH'U (zhiao-khoo)/The Restraining

The image of the wind, gentle (Sun, above), blowing across heaven (Ch'ien, below), suggests restraint of the great power by the small. A strong person is impeded by small, annoying constrictions, forcing him to compromise. A new venture may be impeded by these same forces.

The Judgement

The Restraining Power of the Small: success.
From the west come thick clouds, but no rain.
The prospect of nourishing rain suggests a fruitful outcome, eventually, but clouds prevent it falling. Only through 'the power of the small' — friendly and subtle methods — can we influence others, or events.

The Image

The wind blowing across heaven symbolizes the Restraining Power of the Small.
Thus the superior man refines his character and abilities.
Buffeted by the forces of circumstance, one can achieve little of lasting significance, but conditions allow one to express oneself openly in small ways to those around. One should take the time to develop one's spirit and skills.

The Lines

Nine at the bottom: return to the correct way.
No harm in such a course. Auspicious.
One should not use force, but return to one's previous position and attitude to await a more favourable time. Simply acting in harmony with the nature of the time brings fortune. Anyone now seeking a niche of some sort will find it.

Nine in the second place: he is pressed into returning to the right way. Auspicious.

In pushing forward, one finds oneself alone. Join with others, who are taking a different direction. In this way one can achieve objectives. Promotion is likely.

Nine in the third place: the wagon wheels break away.
A man and his wife argue.

Unaware of trouble looming, one attempts to press forward, but the situation is not able to bear movement, and there is a sudden disruption. Even friends will be unsympathetic and see you as overbearing and crude.

Six in the fourth place: by sincerity bloodshed is averted.
Anxieties vanish. No harm.

Despite prevailing trends, you are close to the centre of events and have some influence. One must first appreciate harsh truths, then take effective action. If you are sensitive and honest, you can correct things and even achieve a small goal.

Nine in the fifth place: if he is sincere and loyal in relationships, he shares the wealth of his neighbours.

Commitment to causes is based on common sympathy and common needs. Selfless co-operation with others bears fruit. Promotion and recognition are likely.

Nine at the top: rain has fallen.
There is peace: one can rest, secure in virtue.
Continuing like a woman brings danger.
The moon is nearly full.
If the superior man advances, misfortune.

The objectionable conditions have passed. But this is no time for complacency for the moon will soon begin to wane. Similarly, the effectiveness of the mild, 'woman' principles begins to diminish, and the hostile elements persist. Do not attempt firm measures. Maintain an impassive attitude and wait.

10. LU (*lu* — as in French *tu*)/Treading

The trigram Ch'ien (the father, above), followed by Tui (the youngest daughter, below), suggests the correct relationship between the two according to Chinese custom. Thus the hexagram advises one to act genteely and in accordance with established conventions.

Alternatively, the bottom trigram's symbolism of a tiger suggests a man treading on the beast's tail. This implies the need for caution in dangerous circumstances and, unusually, the weak being able to presume upon the strong.

The Judgement

Treading. The man steps on a tiger's tail.
It does not bite him. Success.

An unusually intimate proximity of strong and mild elements — this may represent the loner, forced into contact with people he considers lesser than himself. Alternatively, one may be dealing with unpredictable, dangerous forces. Act with pleasant dignity, remaining sensitive.

The Image

Heaven above and the lake below, symbolize Treading.
The superior man discriminates between high and low,
Thus acting in accord with the minds of the people.

The Confucian ideal was a society where outward status was a reflection of inner worth. This idea is perhaps impossible to attain, but one should strive to order behaviour toward others according to a deep appreciation of their nature. Otherwise one can become unrealistic and prejudiced.

The Lines

Nine at the bottom: modest conduct.
Advance without harm.

31

Conscientious and good work is always rewarded in some way. If one is good at what one does, one will advance now. There is a danger of loss of the simple virtue which is the cause of this good fortune.

> *Nine in the second place: treading a smooth, peaceful path.*
> *The quiet, solitary man carries on.*
> *Auspicious.*

One pursues inner goals, unenticed by the lures of the material world. One understands fate and moves contentedly, according to one's inner nature.

> *Six in the third place: the half-sighted man can see; the lame man can walk.*
> *He walks on the tiger's tail: the tiger bites him. Misfortune.*
> *The warrior acts as a prince.*

Like the half-sighted man who believes he has good vision, we are exposing ourselves to all sorts of conflicts and losses. Only a man charged with an urgent or overriding consideration should act so recklessly, and even he is in grave danger.

> *Nine in the fourth place: he treads on the tiger's tail.*
> *Caution and fear.*
> *Auspicious, eventually.*

One is in danger. Trouble threatens both new and established affairs. But with the courage of one's convictions one is able to cautiously move forward.

> *Nine in the fifth place: treading resolutely.*
> *You persevere, aware of danger.*

You are determined, but reckless. There is no easy way out, no quick success is possible. Times are difficult and one may only negotiate safely by being constantly aware of danger.

> *Nine at the top: examine your course, judging well the signs.*
> *If all has been correct, then supreme good fortune.*

Look back at your past way. The end will be good if the way has been good.

☰☷ 11. T'AI (*tie*)/Peace

The leader or father (Ch'ien) supports the people or the mother (K'un). This indicates a strong force creating harmony with the weaker by being flexible and yielding. In general, the hexagram indicates harmonious conditions.

The Judgement

> *Peace. The small is departing,*
> *The great is arriving.*
> *Auspicious: success.*

The strong, creative elements occupy the central position, the lower three lines, and thus are in control. There is a feeling of deep harmony, both in relationships, and circumstances.

The Image

> *Heaven and earth are united, symbolizing Peace.*
> *The king divides and complements the way of heaven and earth.*
> *He observes their phenomena*
> *For the sake of the people.*

Unity produces peace and prosperity. The rulers organize activity according to the appropriate division of time and space so that they may benefit from, and be in harmony with, nature. However mindful you may be of following custom or of 'having someone's best interests at heart', motives can easily become selfish if one does not pay attention to the inner truths which remind one of the universal.

The Lines

Nine at the bottom: when grass is pulled up, its roots come also.
Each sticks to his kind.
Improvement through advancing.

When a man of influence changes his position constructively, he attracts others of like mind. Accept these people, and their help, and work towards common goals. Gains are likely now.

Nine in the second place: tolerating the unevolved, fording the river, neglecting neither friends nor what is far away.
Thus one is able to take the middle way.

When life goes well it is particularly important not to become snobbish or dismissive toward lesser people. One should strictly regulate complacent tendencies and be ready to undertake difficult or unpleasant tasks. Thus one's character and behaviour remain pleasant and correct.

Nine in the third place: no plain without a hill; no going without coming.
Perseverance in dangerous conditions is without blame.
Be not distressed: face reality and enjoy what you have.

Everything is subject to change. Good follows evil and evil follows good. Accept this in your own situation. If conditions seem normal, be cautious and correct or you may find things become worse. If things are bad, remain calm. Contemplate.

Six in the fourth place: he remains cheerful and joins his neighbours without flaunting his advantages.
He is sincere.

You cannot succeed in anything new; you may find yourself at a disadvantage. Deal with others, even rough acquaintances, openly and sincerely.

Six in the fifth place: King I's decree, giving his daughter in marriage.
Consequently, happiness, and great good fortune.

King Wen's father-in-law ordered noble brides to obey their husbands like any other wife, even if they were higher in rank than their spouses. Adjustment by the high to the low, or the strong to the weak, can achieve happiness. A time for promotion, recognition and union.

Six at the top: the walls collapse in the moat.
Use no force, but issue commands in your own town.
Humiliation, if you continue.

Change is occurring, without direct cause from you, or because you have separated activities or relationships without attention to their previous interaction. A town governor might order that a wall be built and a moat dug, without specifying that they be separated by a safe distance. The result could be the wall's collapse. This line indicates trouble of all kinds but one will ameliorate dangerous conditions by a humble, giving attitude.

≡≡ 12. P'I (p-heeh) /Disharmony

Decay, poverty and disjunction are indicated by this hexagram. Here Ch'ien (the leader, strength) above is supported by K'un (the weak, yielding force). No creative result is possible. Thus, it can indicate someone who is strong, loud and arrogant outwardly, but with little inner worth to back up this behaviour.

The Judgement

Disharmony. There is no benefit in this,
Though the superior man perseveres.
The great is departing; the small is arriving.

The creative, ordering forces within situations seem to slip away; confusion and acrimony begin. In general, there is no advantage in action. Concentrate on maintaining affairs humbly and correctly.

The Image

> *Heaven and earth disjoined, symbolizing Disharmony.*
> *Therefore the superior man conceals his true qualities,*
> *Thus avoiding danger,*
> *And shuns favour and fortune.*

In a situation ordered by petty, mean principles and administered by unscrupulous or inferior people, one should not be drawn into involvement for easy gain, be it social or financial.

This hexagram is like the 'Saturn principle' in astrology, or the Taoist idea that 'the seed of prosperity hides within misfortune'. By accepting hardship whilst striving to be pure, one's nature is refined and imperceptibly accrues good fortune.

The Lines

> *Nine at the bottom: when grass is pulled up, its roots come*
>   *also.*
> *Each sticks to his kind.*
> *Perseverance is auspicious.*

Here the tendency is for one to be drawn along towards stagnation or disorder. There may be no harm, and even good, in this. But be cautious in choosing companions. Undertake nothing new, and steer clear of anything remotely unsavoury.

> *Six in the second place: patience and submission.*
> *Auspicious for small people.*
> *The great man continues through hardship. Success.*

Involved with destructive, disordered forces. One should not mix with inferiors or adopt defensive attitudes. If you have strong principles you may suffer for them. Adopt a quiet, humble manner in your dealings.

> *Six in the third place: he is ashamed.*

The leader and those also involved, are ashamed of their

conduct — but will not change. Beware of slander or humiliation.

> *Nine in the fourth place: acting in accord with the highest principles is without blame.*
> *Men of like mind share this blessing.*

Disharmony lessens. Only a bold, principled advance will cause no further harm. Others may be encouraged by this. One may receive benefit from others.

> *Nine in the fifth place: disharmony is fading.*
> *Auspicious for the great man who cries 'Beware, beware!'*
> *He ties it to a mulberry stump.*

The situation can be reversed and order restored. This requires strength and virtue. Restore things carefully and in detail, like tying something down to the many shoots which sprout from the stump of a mulberry bush. Everything may seem well, but one can lose all at this stage.

> *Nine at the top: disharmony ended.*
> *Standstill, then good prospects.*

The end of the tunnel is in sight. There may be difficulties, sorrow and loss. You must make proper efforts to get through. Things will get better.

13. T'UNG JEN (*t-oong zh'n*)/Social Fellowship

The trigram Ch'ien above Li signifies heaven with fire below it: two complementary forces in harmonious relation. The idea of the sun shining brightly in heaven (thus benefiting the farmers in particular, and communities in general) is also indicated. The yielding line in the central place signifies a gentle influence in the midst of men — the wisdom and concern for all which binds men together.

The Judgement

Social Fellowship in the open: success.
Benefit from crossing the great water.
Benefit through the perseverance of the superior man.

The Judgement stresses one's awareness of the constructive principles underlying society, and the unit of social fellowship. This is not a naïve belief, but an understanding that all social co-operation and friendships (despite infinite diversity), require shared goals and common activities. This understanding, when shared, can promote great tasks under the leadership of a principled and organized person.

The Image

Fire reaching heaven, symbolizing Social Fellowship.
Thus the superior man organizes communities,
And distinguishes conditions.

Heaven and fire have different natures, yet both move in the same direction. In order to arrange society, leaders must yield to the diversity of its myriad components, yet organize according to universal principles. The idea of the enormous energy within two forces is stressed here, with the implication that it can easily become uncontrollable.

The Lines

Nine at the bottom: fellowship with others at the gate.
No harm in this.

An image of people inadvertently in each other's company who share common understandings. Co-operate with others and they will reciprocate if the principles are understood. Be honest and open.

Six in the second place: social fellowship within the family.
Regret.

If social contacts are exclusive, snobbishness, unhealthy and quarrelling factions result. Avoid pettiness and shallow discrimination. Be open to others. Loss unlikely, but there may be restrictions and some bitterness.

> *Nine in the third place: hiding weapons in the bushes, he scales a hill.*
> *For three years he hides there.*

A man who mistrusts others and spies on his fellows becomes increasingly alienated from them. Similarly, he cannot fully enter into fellowship with others because of his over-individualistic nature. Mutual mistrust increases and only the humble will do well now.

> *Nine in the fourth place: the defender mounts the wall, but attack is impossible. Auspicious.*

Defensive positions are taken up but the protagonists realize the absurdity of fighting. Difficulties may highlight one's folly, or one may be successful in an undertaking and then encounter difficulties.

> *Nine in the fifth place: forced into fellowship, they weep and complain.*
> *But later they laugh.*
> *Men meet after great battles.*

Generally, conditions are difficult, but improve. A new association may prove wearisome, but easier when one adjusts. On the other hand, lovers parted by circumstances are indicated, with the admonition that inner unity brings union.

> *Nine at the top: fellowship with those in the fields. No guilt.*

The image describes an alliance without inner purpose or warmth. The idea of remoteness suggests that there is no real satisfaction to be gained from one's situation.

14. TA YU (*deh-yuh*)/Possession in Abundance

Fire (Li) in heaven (Ch'ien) symbolizes glory and riches. The yielding line of Li in the position of elevation suggests that great success has been achieved through humility.

The Judgement

Possession in Abundance means supreme success.
The fifth line 'owns' the others — the weak owns the strong through his unselfish virtue. It is a time of regulated, graceful strength and fruition.

The Image

Fire in heaven symbolizes Possession in Abundance.
The superior man, by checking evil and encouraging good,
Is blessed by following the way of heaven's laws.
When one is rich, either in happiness, or wealth, one must conduct oneself no less carefully than when in danger. Otherwise, happiness turns to complacency and bad character produces evil. The sun is high in heaven and begins to wane soon. If one feels that there is something missing, it is a spiritual lack.

The Lines

Nine at the bottom: avoiding the bad; there is no harm in that.
In the end, no mistake, if one sees all the dangers.
Harm is indicated, though there are no overt signs. Wealth is indicated — existing or accruing. By avoiding the coarseness of affluence and by maintaining your principles and sensitivity, you can weather forthcoming difficulties.

Nine in the second place: a great wagon is full.
One may advance without blame.

For some, such a possession is only a burden, restricting freedom. For others, it is the cause and the purpose of mobility. With able helpers one can achieve useful goals now.

Nine in the third place: a great man makes an offering to his king.
A small man could not do this.

Petty people regard wealth selfishly: great people utilize what they have for the good of others. Energetic types may benefit now, though not retiring people.

Nine in the fourth place: he maintains the differences between himself and others without harm.

One should remain unaffected by others' status and wealth, and understand the significance of material divisions between men.

Six in the fifth place: his mobility shines through, tempered with dignity.
Auspicious.

Humanitarian, unselfish attitudes of people often offend by their lack of convention. Thus one should be restrained. The time is favourable, but there is the possibility of trouble with others.

Nine at the top: he is blessed by heaven.
Good fortune. Improvement in every way.

A time of general advance, the supreme honour should be accorded to one who is less worldly. This is the line of thanks in praise of God, of pilgrimage in recognition of good fortune of a modest, virtuous attitude when one is successful.

☶☷ 15. CH'IEN (*Khe-en*) /Modesty

A mountain (Ken) behind earth (K'un) implies a huge

landmark on a great plain. This implies true modesty standing out for all to see. The attribute of Ken as the youngest son of the Creative implies spiritual qualities brought to earth. True modesty functions by examining the situation and one's psyche, and ordering these according to the highest principles. Earth above the mountain also suggests a simple, unglamorous quality elevated in spirit.

The Judgement

Modesty generates success.
The superior man perseveres to the end.

Politeness and modesty generate success and maintain a man once he has wealth or position. The wise man remembers this through the ups and downs of fate.

The Image

A mountain within the earth symbolizes Modesty.
The superior man reduces the excessive,
Increasing that which is deficient:
Thus he weighs and balances.

Mountains are gradually worn down: valleys filled by glaciers and floods. So modesty works imperceptibly, with constancy. For this reason the Chinese regarded modesty more highly than any other virtue.

The wise man, understanding that fate is inescapable, adjusts conditions and himself to avoid extremes, and thus maintains a harmonious life. If this is done from shallow motives the result is petty worry and restriction.

The Lines

Six at the bottom: modest about his virtue, the superior man
can cross the great water. Auspicious.

One free of self-consciousness about his capabilities can achieve great undertakings. The lines suggest new responsibilities and success. If circumstances or instincts say 'no', make no move.

Six in the second place: modesty which expresses itself.
Perseverance is auspicious.
True modesty is evident and profound. By maintaining one's course one will discover opportunities.

Nine in the third place: a superior man works diligently and modestly until the fruition. Good fortune.
The nature of modesty is to succeed through subtle influence. Guard against immodesty if you are successful or have been recognized. Otherwise, unpopularity and demotion will surely follow. Advance is likely for those working in a quiet way.

Six in the fourth place: modesty in action, beneficial in every way.
Modest people, or those in modest positions, can easily use their character or position as an excuse for weakness or vacillation. This weakness is not modesty: it can only sour relations, and make conditions poorer. Act now, taking full account of others. This will lead to significant advances.

Six in the fifth place: no display of wealth before one's neighbours.
Benefit from vigorous attack:
Benefit in everything.
Virtue may be recognized now, though conflict is likely. Take action if the situation demands it, though the necessary steps seem severe. Enlist support if possible.

Six at the top: modesty expressed.
Better to set forces in motion, — even against one's homeland.
Conflicts and difficulties are indicated, but these can be overcome. Start by putting things to right close to home. Painful self-examination may be necessary. Only with ruthless self-knowledge or proper circumstances, can one

achieve success. If successful, guard against squandering the virtues which brought benefit in the first place.

▤ 16. YU (*yiuh*)/Enthusiasm

Chen (thunder, the arousing) above K'un (the earth) indicates enormous creativity or enthusiasm; like powerful music which inspires everyone. The warnings of Yu deal with applying energy without care or preparation. The 'dark side' here is a tendency to use over-forceful methods.

The Judgement

> *Enthusiasm. Improvement through arranging one's affairs,*
> *And setting forces in motion.*

The time is favourable for preparing and starting ventures. The attributes of movement (Chen) and devotion (K'un), suggest that this should be done by support from others and by adjusting one's ideas to their needs. One can thus side-step unseen opposition.

The Image

> *Thunder issues from the earth, symbolizing Enthusiasm.*
> *Thus the king of old composed music in praise of virtue*
> *And offered it with honour to the Absolute,*
> *In the presence of their ancestral spirits.*

Music can soothe emotions and clear tension, just as a recent thunder-storm clears the air. It inspires and moves men through the skill of its composition. This should be in accord with high or metaphysical ideals. The stress on religious ritual here implies that only through a correct interaction between spiritual and material (or idealistic and practical) considerations, can the powerful forces of the time be stabilized.

The Lines

*Six at the bottom: enthusiasm that flaunts itself brings
    misfortune.*
Happiness becomes boorishness if excessively expressed.
Similarly, pride in one's influence can become boasting.
Even good fortune and opportunities will then turn sour.
Benefit is indicated to those modest in manner and life-
style.

Six in the second place: the stability of a rock.
Do not wait one day.
Good fortune if you hold to your way.
One must be as steady as a rock to avoid being trapped in
illusion or swept along by others. But do not hesitate to
act. Retreat or advance, immediately, paying close attention
to the signs of the times. This sensitivity is crucial. Great
improvement is possible.

*Six in the third place: enthusiasm for the higher brings
    regret.*
Hesitation brings regret.
You may be waiting for approval from your boss, a loved
one, someone you admire, or for a 'sign from heaven' in
some form. Don't! You will be left behind. Indeed, this may
already be happening. Anticipate rapid progress or decline
and act accordingly.

Nine in the fourth place: the font of enthusiasm.
One achieves great things: no doubt about it.
Friends are drawn, as a comb gathers hair.
One who can inspire others by his influence and sureness,
draws others to him like hairs through the teeth of a comb.
One succeeds, and others share the benefit.

Six in the fifth place: chronically ill, still alive.
One feels restricted, burdened with persistent problems,
unable to express one's ideas or put them into effective
action. No advance, though one might gain through others.

Six at the top: mindless enthusiasm.
But if the cycle ends and one changes one's course, there is
no harm.

If carried away by enthusiasm for its own sake you will inevitably run into trouble. Come down from this artificial high as soon as possible or a rude awakening awaits.

17. SUI (*sweah*)/Following

Above is Tui (the youngest daughter, the joyous) and below is Chen (the eldest son, the arousing). Suggests an older man deferring to a young girl. The attributes of the trigrams also suggest someone who is full of creative power and appears happy and pleasant.

The Judgement

Following brings supreme success.
Benefit in perseverance: no harm in this.

In order to become a powerful leader, one must adapt to the demands of others, however foolish or unnecessary. By treating others cynically one becomes frustrated and causes conflicts. One should persevere in order to retain harmony and confidence amongst one's supporters.

The Image

Thunder in the lake, symbolizing Following.
The superior man withdraws at nightfall
And rests at home.

The autumn (Sui) indicates a fading of the bright and strong. This is a time of easy gain and loss, tending toward loss. Adapt, conserving your efforts.

The Lines

Nine at the bottom: the condition changes.

Persevering is auspicious.
To go out and mingle produces good effects.
The relationship between a man and his friends is changing. As leader he should adapt to their needs, but do what is right. However, the circle of friendship, or activity, is too much of a clique, with all that implies.

Six in the second place: if you stay with the little boy, you lose the great man.
One should distinguish between rules and behaviour applicable to an intimate situation, and those with wider implications. One may have to choose between remaining — and so missing an opportunity — or leaving.

Six in the third place: if you stay with the great man, you lose the little boy.
One finds one's goal through following.
Benefit from perseverance.
By choosing the more significant or 'higher' path, one loses the familiar. But stick to your aim. Gain is likely if your conduct is proper.

Nine in the fourth place: success by following.
Misfortune from continuing.
Sincerity leads to brightness. No Harm.
If one has attracted success through one's influence, one should examine it and resultant relationships carefully. Perhaps one's ego is swollen. If all seems correct, good fortune through others is likely.

Nine in the fifth place: confidence in what is good.
Auspicious.
This line indicates constancy, correctness or an unshakable ambition. Promotion and success are indicated.

Six at the top: he is bound by faithfulness.
He is presented in the temple of Western Mountain.
A place in the royal family's temple was seen as the highest honour — but only when dead. The line indicates one who

47

would rather retire from his position. One should guard against loss, conflict or illness.

18. KU (*giuh*)/Reparation of the Spoiled

Sun (the wind, below) tears at the foot of the mountain (Ken). This implies destruction: grass and bushes uprooted, orchards ruined. But the time indicated by spring (Sun) following the winter (Ken) indicates change. Hard work is indicated. In settled businesses, communities, relationships, etc., Sun indicates fundamentally bad or incompatible arrangements.

The Judgement

Reparation of the Spoiled brings supreme success.
Benefit from crossing the great water.
Three days duration before starting.
Three days after starting.

Ku indicates present or imminent loss and trouble. The cause is largely one's own attitudes and behaviour. One has either been confused and ignored responsibilities, or been dishonest and ambiguous. Ruin seems unavoidable. This is precisely why this is considered an auspicious hexagram. This is the time for decisive and energetic action, to repair the damage done. It is imperative to consider and contemplate before, and after, beginning.

The Image

Wind blowing at the foot of the mountain symbolizes
  Spoiling.
Therefore the superior man encourages the people
To fortify their virtue.

When all is destroyed, or in danger of destruction, the wise man works hard at orderly reorganization. People and relationships must be activated, then solid, virtuous conditions established.

The Lines

Six at the bottom: the ruin brought about by the father is repaired by the son.
If he succeeds, no blame upon the father.
Danger, but the end is auspicious.

By unquestioning or narrow adherence to outmoded standards, or habitual principles, one is unable to react honestly or effectively to the present. Decay has started, but it can be corrected before it affects everyone. But the necessary reform carries its own dangers — especially carelessness, which would have far-reaching effects.

Nine in the second place: in repairing the ruin brought about by the mother, do not be too persistent.

Serious weaknesses have led to this situation. A change of outlook is called for.

Nine in the third place: repairing what was ruined by his father.
Some remorse, but no harm done.

Over-enthusiastic correction of past mistakes leads to errors and criticism.

Six in the fourth place: overlooking the ruin brought about by one's father.
Continuing brings regret.

Things have begun to deteriorate. Because you overlook symptoms or their cause things will get steadily worse. There is still time to correct faults, but many are one's own, and run deep.

Six in the fifth place: repairing what was ruined by his father,
He is praised.

Reform brings warmth from relieved friends and colleagues. A time of advanced and perhaps new undertakings.

> *Nine at the top: not serving kings and princes, he cultivates higher ambitions.*

Many will view the past with distaste, or will see nothing wrong now. Concentrate on higher aspirations, but do not relax. Not a time for individual undertakings.

☷☱ 19. LIN *(lin)*/Conduct

Tui, the youngest daughter below, or behind K'un, the mother, indicates the image of kindly authority, and the correct relationship between two people, one 'above' the other.

The Judgement

> *Conduct: great success,*
> *Benefit by continuing.*
> *Ominous, when the eighth month comes.*

A time of good fortune: the solid ascending lines indicate growth and energy. But the warning of the eighth month is that one should be prepared, guard one's conduct and pay constant attention to the signs of the times.

The Image

> *The lake within the earth, symbolizing Conduct (fertility).*
> *Thus the superior man is inexhaustibly nourished,*
> *And inexhaustibly he nourishes the people.*

The earth above the lake indicates the elevated position of one, and a superior attitude toward another. The correct course is to educate by example and through concern for what is below.

The Lines

Nine at the bottom: approach with another.
Good fortune in perseverance.

A time of improvement, if one does not get carried away by the signs of favour coming one's way. Promotion and success are likely. Seek authoritative help if possible.

Nine in the second place: approach with another.
Improvement in everything.

This indicates one who is cheerful, has the strength and will to succeed, and understands the laws of life. A fortunate time.

Six in the third place: careless approach. Futile.
If one can become anxious, there is no harm.

Once in a comfortable position, one becomes careless and offensive. If one changes this attitude, all will be well. A time of worry, or sadness, with no great advance.

Six in the fourth place: open conduct. No harm.

Harmonious conditions, favour from above, and success for working people are indicated.

Six in the fifth place: wise conduct, suitable for a noble.
Auspicious.

A leader must be wise in delegation. Thus one should study the characters of those useful or important to oneself. A time of smooth achievement.

Six at the top: honest and generous conduct is auspicious.
No harm in this.

This implies returning to something or someone left, to pass on the benefit of his experience. The line implies success or harmony.

☴☷ 20. KUAN (*gw'n*)/View

The wind (Sun) above the earth (K'un) suggests wind

blowing dust around, or the useless efforts of air (mental activity) to arrange earth (material things). It is not a time to undertake anything new but, rather, to settle down in one's affairs, just as farmers of old during the time of Kuan (late September to mid-October) would store their harvests and begin the long business of mending tools and preparing for the next year.

The Judgement

Meditation. The ablution is done,
but not yet the sacrifice.
The people look up, full of respect.

The moment between ritual washing and sacrifice is indicated. Those in charge of projects, or those who influence others, must have great sensitivity towards their responsibilities.

The hexagram shape, which is like an ancient gatetower, also symbolizes the Tao — the Way, along (or through) which all life must work out its existence. It intensifies the ideas of contemplation, for the Tao serves as a symbol to all, like the watchers at the sacrifice, respectfully looking upward. Thus the subject is not only someone who meditates (or, more mundanely, someone who looks widely or deeply into things) but also that which is contemplated.

The Image

Wind over the earth, symbolizing View.
Thus superior men travel boundlessly,
Meditating upon the people of the world,
And teaching them.

This refers to the tours made by Chinese rulers to 'get close to the grass roots' (contemplate), and exercise influence (be contemplated by the people). A strong, influential and wise man is, by deep and unprejudiced enquiry, able to bring great benefit. This is, again, a general symbol of the Tao, the gateway of 'the eternal present' and the symbol of clarity and balance.

The Lines

Six at the bottom: his view is like an urchin's.
For inferior people, no blame; for superior ones, regret.
A shallow view cannot understand virtue, or superior men. This is unimportant for people whose actions are guided by a wise leader. This is a time of unrealistic thinking, great activity, but little success.

Six in the second place: view through a crack in the door.
Benefit from persevering in woman's ways.
A narrow, self-centred view, is indicated. This is only appropriate to women's household activity. It is better to engage in humble and gentle activities now. A time of difficulty in work requiring concentration.

Six in the third place: viewing one's own life, one thus
*   chooses advance or retreat.*
Self-contemplation is indicated. This should not be confused with worried egotism, though one may be guilty of this. Objective self-examination is the key to decision. A time of ups and downs. Work with caution.

Six in the fourth place: viewing the glory of the country.
Benefit comes from knowing, and influencing the ruler.
Someone is indicated whose balanced view of past and future, or of the form and content of structures (for instance, the organization of a national establishment) gives him a valuable understanding of social processes and he should be honoured, not treated as a subordinate. One may benefit from travel or be promoted.

Nine in the fifth place: view of the self.
No harm, for the superior man.
A balanced, equable but selfish view is indicated. Promotion is likely; independent success too. To counteract

selfishness one should strive to create good in everything one does.

Nine at the top: view of life.
The superior man is blameless.

One who excludes personal feelings is indicated — possibly a wise, strong man or one whose unemotional stance deludes him about his ability to 'transcend' life's ugly realities. Here is the difference between the superior man, and the emotional poseur. A time of difficulties and no advance, but perhaps recuperation.

21. SHIH HO (*sh'rr ho'r*) /Biting Through

The characteristics of Li (lightning, above) and Chen (thunder, below) are combined here. The hexagram shape suggests vigorous chewing (which bites through obstacles). As this imagery suggests, Shih Ho indicates trouble or difficulties at the beginning.

The Judgement

Biting: success.
Benefit from the administration of justice.

The shape of the hexagram suggests an open mouth with an obstacle between the teeth. Thus the Judgement indicates an obstacle to union or harmony, and thus the necessity to 'bite through' to remove it. The attributes of the trigrams indicate the balance which must be achieved in 'administering justice'. Li, the Clinging, is yielding, whilst Chen, the Arousing, is hard. One's actions, though vigorous, must not be hasty, severe, or arbitrary, but carefully considered to encompass all the circumstances.

The Image

Thunder and lightning; the image of Biting Through.

> *Thus the kings would make laws firm by clearly defining consequences.*

Movement starts from below with thunder (difficulties). Lightning symbolizes the clarity with which the rules and nature of the situation must be perceived, according to the quality of the times.

The Lines

> *Nine at the bottom: his feet in the stocks, so the toes disappear. No blame.*

It is a time of loss, demotion or even punishment for past 'crimes', real or imagined. In relationships, persistent dishonesty is beginning to undermine bonds between the parties. With caution and care, the situation can be saved, if not fully restored.

> *Six in the second place: he bites through tender meat, his nose disappears. No harm.*

One is wronged, or has to make a choice to right a wrong. The choice is easy enough, but if one's anger is aroused by the apparently unmitigated badness of things, the result will be over-reaction.

> *Six in the third place: biting on stored meat, he encounters something rotten.*
> *Minor regret, but no harm in this.*

The meat symbolizes a problem that is old or tough. By dealing with it one will attract vituperation, but one's actions, if correct, will be accepted in the end. Success if hampered now — failures and criticisms are likely.

> *Nine in the fourth place: he bites on stored, bony meat; receives coins and weapons.*
> *Benefit in recognizing difficulties, and in persevering. Auspicious.*

Great difficulties and powerful opponents must be overcome. You should be hard. However, it is a time of gain. Do not be excessive.

Six in the fifth place: biting on lean stored meat, he
encounters gold.
Keeping his way, recognizing danger. No harm.
Habitual leniency can be ineffective and real problems may
occur. Not using the law correctly undermines the stability
of a society; not following your principles positively and
with restraint undermines your character. Therefore, if you
have responsibilities, meet them. A profitable time.

Nine at the top: the man's neck locked under the yoke, his
ears out of sight. Unfortunate.
This refers to an incorrigible rogue. Deaf to warnings, he
has allowed small evils to accumulate. The result is
imminent demotion, conflicts, slander and widespread
unpopularity from all quarters. One could even lose one's
job.

☶ 22. PI (*bee*)/Gracefulness

Ken, the upper trigram, means mountain; Li, below, is fire,
brightness or sun. Hence the image of the sun shining on
the foot of the mountain, illuminating all. The same idea of
illumination is contained in the symbol of fire on the
mountain. The personal attributes of Ken and Li —
respectively, the youngest son and the middle daughter —
indicate a young couple. These images imply beauty and
energy which must be regulated by aesthetic sensitivity if it
is to last. The union of a youth with a woman who will
reach middle age whilst he is still young and irresponsible
warns against taking beauty or permanency for granted.

The Judgement

Gracefulness: success in small undertakings.
The structure of the hexagram emphasizes form, rather than
content. Thus, only small undertakings are favoured.

Chinese commentators have pointed to the accompanying idea of contemplation or clarity (stakes associated with a beautiful or pleasing object) whilst stressing that art is only icing on the cake of reality. It has nothing to do with the basic, essential conditions of one's life.

The Image

> *A fire burning at the mountain's edge symbolizes*
> *Gracefulness.*
> *Thus the superior man clarifies everyday issues,*
> *But dares not judge great proceedings.*

Matters of unenduring importance can be ordered to advantage, but no great affairs or changes should be undertaken. Aesthetics and grace will help in everyday matters.

The Lines

> *Nine at the bottom: he adorns his toes, dismisses his*
> *carriage, and walks.*

This image of walking indicates the practical necessity to advance from a humble position, without assuming pretentious airs. One should expect to be active, perhaps travel, and meet difficulties.

> *Six in the second place: he cultivates his beard.*

Attending to one's beard (an ornament) indicates petty self-consciousness. Remember, form is only a result of deeper, more serious matters. Do not become so involved in superficialities as to make them appear pretentious. An auspicious time for receiving help.

> *Nine in the third place: elegant and moist.*
> *Continuing in perseverance is auspicious.*

This line represents one 'moist' with drink. When enjoying a peaceful and mellow situation, one should neither neglect one's more material responsibilities, nor should undue effort be directed toward prolonging one's pleasure. A time of easy, if undramatic success.

Nine in the fourth place: elegance or simplicity?
A white horse, arriving as though winged.
He does not bear a robber but a serious suitor.

One is torn between the attractions of widespread popularity, (making one feel successful, though rather 'lost') and the simple, close communication with one, or a few, special friends. The winged horse, symbolizing simplicity and the transcendent power of love, indicates that there are exterior signs which point toward a simpler life-style.

Six in the fifth place: gracefulness in the hills and
*   gardens.*
His roll of silk is poor.
First regret, then good fortune.

Seeking a 'higher' way of life, entering a new milieu, one finds difficulty at first. But empathy and sincerity are more important than material equality, and all goes well eventually. Not a time of major successes.

Nine at the top: simple gracefulness. No harm.

A balanced condition, where form and content are in recognizable unity. One should stick to simple undertakings, which will be successful.

23. PO
(po'r)/Disintegration

Po represents decay, dissolution and misfortune. The season indicated is autumn, when everything is beginning to rot and disintegrate. The five yin lines suggest weak, dark forces moving up to overcome the strong. The shape of the hexagram suggests a house with only walls and roof remaining. The structure is there, but is ready to collapse.

The Judgement

Disintegration.
No benefit in any action.
The creative force (the yang line), is about to be supplanted by the disorderly elements below. It is a time of misfortune. Direct any efforts towards others, one's own affairs are badly augered.

The Image

The mountain on the earth symbolizes Disintegration.
Superior men can maintain themselves.
Only through benevolence to the inferior.
Ken, the mountain, stands exposed to the wearing blasts of nature upon K'un, the earth. Bear problems with dignity, maintain virtue by selfless behaviour. The situation cannot be advanced, but, with absolute rectitude, one may save it from disaster.

The Lines

Six at the bottom: the legs of the couch disintegrate.
This way brings destruction. Ominous.
One can only wait. Perhaps unfair, certainly powerful, conditions threaten to bring ruin if you act. In any case you have no choice.

Six in the second place: the frame of the couch disintegrates.
This way brings destruction. Ominous.
The rise of the inferior and dangerous continues. Signs of imminent disaster. One must take prompt action, but the circumstances may prove overwhelming, despite one's best efforts.

Six in the third place: he is among those who overturn the couch.

No blame.

Recognizing the evil yet bound to it, one should seek to compromise, or take an unusual and unexpected exit. There is no blame attached to this.

> *Six in the fourth place: the couch is overturned, bruising its*
>   *occupant. Misfortune.*

Misfortune can no longer be avoided.

> *Six in the fifth place: like a bunch of fish.*
> *Favour through the women of the royal household.*
> *Improvements in everything.*

The top, weak line, leading the others like fish on a line, subordinates itself to the strong, leading element like women-in-waiting before their mistress. Success and recognition are indicated.

> *Nine at the top: a large fruit, not yet eaten.*
> *The superior man is carried as if by a chariot.*
> *The house of the inferior man distintegrates.*

Good fortune through being correct and careful. The misfortune has spent itself, and the 'fruit' you will receive is yours to eat. The superior person finds his influence growing, and is supported by others. The inferior man, unable or unwilling to learn from his experiences, finds that worse disaster befalls him. The message is: understand and be sensitive to all experiences. The seeds of your future lie within the flow of recent events. Take them, but do not cling to the useless husks of previous ideals and ambitions.

24. FU (*f'uh*)/Returning

Fu, linked with the winter solstice, the point of lowest vitality, indicates a decrease in bad fortune. The single unbroken line at the bottom represents the warm, creative yang force rising. The lower trigram Chen (wood) within K'un (earth) symbolizes the roots of a plant. Hence we have the idea of imminent growth, new opportunities, and potential success.

The Judgement

Returning: success.
There is no mistake in going out and entering again.
Friends enter without harm.
The course of the Tao is to and fro.
On the seventh day, returning.
There is benefit in one's undertaking.

After the creative forces retreat, they return. In human affairs those of like mind and character join harmoniously together in new undertakings. This mirrors the movement of the Tao. The seventh stage is that of return; a new cycle after the old.

The Image

Thunder within the earth symbolizes Returning.
Thus, in ancient times the kings closed the passes at the winter solstice.
Merchants and travellers ceased their travels,
And rulers did not visit their provinces.

The principle of rest, whilst the life energy is held within the earth, means that everything must be treated carefully and must not be hurried. One cannot force a bud to open: one can, and must, however, prepare the soil for its future growth. Good prospects for established affairs, although the time is less suitable for entirely new projects.

The Lines

Nine at the bottom: returning from the near, no indication of guilt.
Greatly auspicious.

One has begun to stray from the true path, and should

correct this minor digression before it leads to greater evil. A time of material rewards.

Six in the second place: quiet return is auspicious.
An air of excitement, creativity, or a sense of the imminent is noticed. Be alive to the new influence and to others' creative ideas, even if it means swallowing your pride.

Six in the third place: returning again and again.
Danger, but no guilt.
This is the line of 'two steps forward, three steps back'. It indicates one whose insecurity prompts constant neglect of his way forward and may even cause obvious steps back. This does not harm others, and the weakness is reversible. Changing conditions, with no great successes or failures are indicated.

Six in the fourth place: one walks amongst others yet
returns alone.
A change for the better — perhaps not obvious to others — may prompt you to action. This may alienate you from others, but is certainly for the best.

Six in the fifth place: honourable return. No guilt.
If faults must be faced, so be it. If confession is demanded, it must be given. One's reaction will be influential. Success is indicated, though minor losses are possible.

Six at the top: confused return, misfortune, deep disaster.
Forces set in motion would suffer a massacre: the ruler
would be defeated, and unable to govern for ten years.
An opportunity has come and gone and has been missed. One can do nothing now without making matters ten times worse. A quiet, humble and repentent attitude is the best and proper way now.

☰ 25. WU WANG (*w'u w'ng*) ☷ /Simplicity

From Ch'ien (above) comes the attribute of creative, heavenly law: below, is Chen — movement and strength. Thus we have the idea of energy following the laws of heaven; a natural and happy state of affairs. This is a time of undertakings.

The Judgement

Simplicty: supreme success.
Perseverance brings benefit.
If one is not as one should be, then ominous.
There is no benefit in
Any of one's undertakings.

The purity and goodness of genuine innocence brings success when one perseveres, because one's way is in accord with the movement of higher forces. If one merely seems natural and good-hearted or if one tempers one's instinct with 'political' or practical compromises, there is little advantage to be gained, and one progressively loses touch with one's own way.

The Image

Thunder rolling beneath heaven symbolizes Simplicity.
This is the quality of everything.
Thus, once, kings of timely virtue
Cared for their subjects and nourished the state, in
harmony with the natural condition.

Life energies begin to emerge again at the start of spring and then nourish their affairs accordingly. The idea of thunder in spring indicates an extra possibility — sudden difficulties, or unexpected changes in conditions. The fundamental force now is creative and growing. Thus troubles should not be artificially removed, but one should adapt, as naturally and guilelessly as possible.

The Lines

Nine at the bottom: acting wth simplicity. Auspicious.
A time of harmony and good fortune. One should follow, confidently and simply, the directions of one's inner voice.

Six in the second place: the superior man does not measure the harvest whilst ploughing, nor the crop from a bare field.
There is benefit in advance.
A time of advance in the right time and place (exams, for instance, being regular and anticipated events, are a typical example). Elsewhere, one should fulfil one's responsibilities as they occur, and complete every task because it should be completed, not because of anticipated rewards.

Six in the third place: unexpected calamity.
The tethered ox is taken: the wanderer's gain is the villagers' misfortune.
Profit for some, loss for others is indicated here. Elsewhere, accept disappointments, though others may see them as especially unfair.

Nine in the fourth place: in persevering simplicity, there is no mistake.
If true to our essential natures, we can make no mistake. Within this inscrutable ideal lies one of the most valuable philosophies of the *I Ching*. A time of moderate, though unspectacular success.

Nine in the fifth place: the unexpected illness will not be cured with medicine.
It will cure itself simply.
The line indicates a sudden misfortune which affects you

deeply. One should now, more than ever, retain clear simplicity within, and should not invent easy solutions or ingenious plans. React spontaneously and freely and things will clear up. A time of success, even if difficulties ensnare you at first.

Nine at the top: simplicity in action is disastrous.
No benefit.

The time is not right for further progress, so do not simply blunder on. Do not trust your instincts. One may need cunning to deal with tricky situations.

26. TA CH'U (*deh kh'oo*) /Great Power in Restraint

Ta Ch'u protrays the active power of heaven (Ch'ien, below) trapped within stillness (Ken). Thus we have a situation of great potential force — just as a river restrained within dam walls produces energy. The main meanings attributed to this hexagram, are the ideas of great reserves of energy; of great restraint upon a creative force; and of a source of nourishment (which may be spiritual and practical or material).

The Judgement

Great Power in Restraint: benefit in perseverance.
Not eating at home brings advancement;
It is auspicious to cross the great water.

The imagery points to a great deal of work ahead. The quality of the time (restrained power) points to storing one's energies and conserving one's virtue by constant effort, together with some useful discipline, such as meditation. When physical and psychic energies are in harmony, one can remain in tune with the flux of external forces, so even great undertakings have every chance of success.

The Image

Heaven within the mountain symbolizes Great Power in Restraint.

Thus the superior man studies the wisdom and the great deeds of the ancients.

Thus he improves his character.

Two broad meanings are indicated here: one refers to that which is stored, be it material wealth, or enduring truths ('the wisdom of the ancients'), the other indicates a person who has either absorbed the acquiescence of those around and should now beware of becoming complacent, or needs to gain others' confidence to achieve success.

The Lines

Nine at the bottom: meeting danger, one must halt.

Difficulties may mean halt or even retreat. Advance or continuing on one's present course, will certainly bring misfortune. Wait for a more harmonious time and be content with small improvements.

Nine in the second place: the bracket of the wagon breaks away.

Opposed by a superior force, halt or retreat is imperative. Struggle is simply impossible. Therefore, conserve your energies. Advancement through another's efforts is possible.

Nine in the third place: good horses working together.

Perseverance, recognizing difficulties, brings benefits.

One practises horsemanship and martial arts each day.

There is benefit in advancing towards an objective.

Current conditions or other people are moving in the same direction as oneself, but one must remain careful of dangerous obstacles ahead. Keep your aim firmly in mind, planning sensible alternatives in case the path is blocked. A time of advancement through hard work.

Six in the fourth place: a horn-shield on the young bull.
Greatly fortunate.

The wild power of a young bull was neutralized by covering the horns with a wooden board before they became dangerous. Similarly, with foresight, one can forestall even great danger or difficulties and achieve one's goals. A time of potential success.

Six in the fifth place: the tusks of a castrated boar.
Auspicious.

A dangerous force is neutralized here by removing the cause of the danger, not its symptoms. A time of good fortune and recognition.

Nine at the top: he succeeds in the way of heaven. Success.
The creative energy, so long restrained, now emerges triumphantly and exercises enormous influence. A time of promotion, recognition, and wide-ranging success.

27. I (*y'ee*)/Nourishment

Beneath the trigram Ken (stillness) is Chen (movement). The fixed above and moving below, (with the hexagram shape, which suggests an open mouth) gives I the attribute of a mouth, through which nourishment passes. Since plants and herbs growing at the foot of the mountain (Ken is the mountain, Chen is wood or vegetable matter) are amongst the most nourishing, the idea is reinforced. The imagery of thunder (Chen) rolling around the base of the mountain indicates that nourishing rain will soon fall. The warnings within I refer to achieving harmony and maintaining moderation (for immoderate eating will surely lead, at least, to discomfort).

The Judgement

Nourishment: perseverance is auspicious.

Give attention to providing nourishment,
And the nourishment
One seeks for himself.

The idea is expanded to include one's nourishing of others
— be this literal or metaphorical, material or spiritual. When
nourishing oneself or others one must be careful to
discriminate between that which is pure and life-enhancing,
and that which is unworthy.

The Image

Thunder at the foot of the mountain, symbolizing
  Nourishment.
The superior man is careful of his words,
And cautious in eating and drinking.

The mouth is a modifying medium: it chews food, shapes
words and is in constant motion. A great deal of work is
indicated with the suggestion that difficult conditions or
people should be cultivated and tamed. Later they will be
useful.

The Lines

Nine at the bottom:
You can release your magic tortoise and look at me slackly.
Ominous.

One who ignores the example of the oracle tortoise (which
were considered divine, and without need of food) is in
danger of losing his self-reliance or independence. He
becomes envious of others and so incurs misfortune. A
time of conflict due to criticism of one's behaviour. People
working unobtrusively, however, will not be adversely
affected.

Six in the second place: he seeks nourishment from the top,
  turning from the correct path onto the hill.
Acting in this fashion brings misfortune.

If one who is normally self-reliant, or has a regular source of income or 'nourishment', cannot support himself, or turns away to another source, he begins to shirk basic responsibilities and evil soon results. This is a time of good and bad fortune. Even the virtuous cannot be sure which way things will go — but the effects will not be excessive.

Six in the third place: turning away from nourishment is ominous if one continues.
One should not behave thus for ten years. No advance.

Misconduct rather than correct bearing, junk foods rather than wholefood, selfish gratification rather than open, selfless enjoyment — these and other types of foolish preferences should never become more than isolated excursions. Poor fortunes and decline may be due to one's own misconduct.

Six in the fourth place: seeking nourishment from the summit brings good fortune.
Staring around like a starved tiger: no mistakes here.

This could be a time of gain or loss, depending on other forces. The line refers to one who seeks help in a worthy enterprise, or who is alert to favourable circumstances. Alternatively, one in a responsible position, acting correctly, but looking for others to support him, may be indicated.

Six in the fifth place: turning from the path.
Auspicious, but he should not cross the great water.

Conscious of personal deficiencies or surrounding conditions, one changes direction, acting, perhaps, unconventionally. If one has insufficient strength to help others, one should change one's tack and seek influential or wise help. One should not undertake any great ventures.

Nine at the top: the source of nourishment.
Circumspect, thus auspicious conditions.
Great benefit in crossing the great water.

One is indicated here who is in harmony with his sources of nourishment, whatever they are. Likewise, he nourishes others. If aware of the responsibilities of his position, he can continue indefinitely. Good fortune and success are indicated.

≣ 28. TA KUO (*daih gwoh*) /Excessive Greatness

The shape of the hexagram represents a thick and heavy beam, which is weak at the ends. Thus it has no firm support. The two trigrams, Tui (water or lake, above) and Sun (wood or tree, below) suggest trees under water — a flood. This specifically indicates excess, and with the idea derived from the hexagram's shape, presents the picture of a dangerous situation which must not continue.

The Judgement

Excessive Greatness: the beam is bowed and will collapse.
There is benefit in advancing toward objectives. Success.
The image suggests the seriousness of the time. Various situations are suggested — business affairs or emotional relationships may be over-complex. Although troubles are almost inevitable, strong lines in the centre of Ta Kuo show the ability of the subject to withstand oncoming difficulties. The solidity of this hexagram insists that the way to solve the problems (insofar as they are soluble) is by a gentle application of the understanding.

The Image

The lake rising over the trees symbolizes Excessive Greatness.
Therefore, the superior man stands alone, unworried.
If he must withdraw from the world, he is without regret.

The attitude the wise man takes is indicated. Though alone, one must be firm like the tree (Sun, below), without losing an open, joyous attitude to life (Tui, the joyous, above). The flood image reinforces one aspect of the situation — flood waters must drain away: the troubles will be temporary.

Remember that, however pleasant or profitable things are now, they will not last.

The Lines

Six at the bottom: spreading rush mats beneath.
No mistake here.

By diligence and hard, sensitive planning, you have a chance to advance as you choose. But, just as one spreads mats under fragile pots, it is important to be especially cautious in all one's affairs.

Nine in the second place: new shoots sprouting from the withered willow.
The older man takes a young wife.
Improvement in every way.

A time of rejuvenation and advancement. The image of the newly-shooting tree which grows near water suggests one has tapped a previously forgotten or neglected source of nourishment (material or otherwise). Unusual liaisons and partnerships are favoured.

Nine in the third place: the beam bends almost to breaking.
Ominous.

Anyone who ignores the signs of approaching peril, or who is stubborn, will have certain trouble. The habit of pushing ahead, of 'pressing on regardless', has caught up with the subject of this line.

Nine in the fourth place: the beam is braced. Auspicious.
But looking for more support brings deep regret.

One succeeds in mastering the situation through the help

of others. Abusing their trust, or making further demands, will lead to a fall. A compliant manner will help smooth daily affairs. One can expect recognition or promotion if it is proper.

Nine in the fifth place: flowers blossoming from the withered willow.
An older woman takes a young husband.
No mistakes here, no recognition.

Essentially, things are barren and repressed. A time of difficulty. One should take care to preserve fairness and balance in one's affairs and relationships.

Six at the top: forced to cross the stream, it covers his head.
Misfortune, but no blame attached.

Pressing blindly on without due regard for the nature of the situation has brought trouble. You hurt only yourself. A time of sadness.

☵ 29. K'AN (khunn)/The Deep

K'an, two primary trigrams of the same name, means danger, crisis and involvement in conflict. Literally, it is 'double-danger'. It can indicate an attitude to life, such as that shown by the sort of person who must constantly face, or create crises in order to give meaning to life. More commonly, it indicates a dangerous situation to which one must adjust. Danger means that through which one can be hurt, but it can also mean advancement and inner development, if one behaves correctly.

The Judgement

The Deep repeated: sincerity means success, harmony in one's spirit.
From this comes success in all you do.

Like water flowing onwards wherever possible, sincerity

enables us to understand the deepest part of a situation, and take effective action. Danger strengthens the spirit, and reinforces the awareness that inner peace is the most important ingredient of success. With calm within, one can move quickly forward to avoid disaster.

The Image

> *Water pours from the deep unceasingly; symbolizing the*
> *Deep repeated.*
> *Therefore the superior man maintains his virtue always,*
> *And continues his practice of teaching.*

Water, in an endless stream, symbolizes the wise approach to virtue. One should ensure that virtue permeates one's life and that it is of sufficient calibre to cope with the most distressing and unusual conditions. One should improve oneself constantly and avoid selfishness by influencing others with one's own virtue.

The Lines

> *Six at the bottom: deep upon deep.*
> *Caught in this, he stumbles into a pit. Misfortune.*

You have become used to danger and so you have become indifferent, and have lost your feeling for the right way. One who lacks purpose, awareness, or defensiveness now may be demoted or severely reprimanded.

> *Nine in the second place: dangers of the deep.*
> *Small relief through small achievements.*

Weigh up the situation, and try not to make a precipitous escape. Difficult conditions must be endured, but small undertakings will help.

> *Six in the third place: at every turn, depth upon depth.*
> *Danger everywhere; cease struggling and wait, or you will*
> *fall into the gaping pit.*
> *Do not act thus.*

Danger is present. Any reaction will increase the trouble. Inaction is imperative until a clear way out is revealed. Those with a quiet life-style should work hard and humbly; those playing active parts in any situation should expect severe conflicts.

Six in the fourth place: a jug of wine, two bowls of rice.
Simple vessels, passed through the window. No blame.

Sincerity is stressed through the image of the simplest possible ceremony in passing over traditional gifts given by one provincial official to another. Sincerity becomes more important than ritual or custom in difficult times, and everything proceeds from that clear, simple, contact at the beginning. A time of increasing status or friendly meeting, and, also, a time of possible sadness.

Nine in the fifth place: the deep is near overflowing.
But it is filled only to the rim.
No mistake in this.

In order to escape from danger, one need only take the line of least resistance, just as liquid spills from a vessel over the lowest point of its rim. Concentrate only on escaping. Other difficulties are too numerous now. A time when one may achieve goals smoothly, if conditions are settled.

Six at the top: bound with many ropes, he is thrown into the thorn-thickets gaol.
For three years he is blind to the way which means freedom.
Ominous.

This line indicates entanglement, and restraint, be it physical (prison, or a crippling fine, for instance) or abstract (perhaps a despised job, or a disliked person). One is the victim of one's misdeeds — trapped like a criminal after losing the way of heaven, hampered and restrained with bad luck for an extended, through not permanent, period.

☲ 30. LI (*lee*)/Fire

The trigram Li (brightness, fire, clinging) repeated makes this hexagram. The doubling of those qualities can mean simply a fiery, short-tempered person, or an explosive, unstable situation. It can also refer to clinging. Clinging is an attribute of fire. It clings to that on which it feeds, whilst radiating its glory everywhere. In particular terms, Li here could refer to, say, a quarrelsome, energetic person (a successful self-made businessman perhaps) or an assertive male lover, whose demanding, loud affections are a cover (consciously or not) for his dependence on someone else. The moral is that motivating energy, like fire, must be controlled for it to be constructive, and to avoid it becoming destructive.

The Judgement

Perseverance brings benefit: success.
Tending the cow is auspicious.

The outgoing energy, symbolized by fire, is constantly being used up. Therefore it must have some enduring inner source, otherwise it will die. Perseverance is indicated by the image of the docile cow. It is important for a fiery person to acknowledge dependence (just as a cow depends upon the farmer) and it is also important for him to become more amenable in his behaviour, in order to develop clarity and understanding. This is a vital antidote to excessive behaviour and attitudes.

The Image

The bright quality repeated, symbolizing Fire.
Thus great men refine brilliance.
To illuminate even unto the world's darkest places.

The sun-like attributes of Li, doubled, emphasizes cyclic time and regularity. Thus one should deliberately and regularly refine the clear, energetic quality which is indicated, so that its influence spreads without limit.

The Lines

Nine at the bottom: jumbled footprints.
With composure, no harm.
Early morning is indicated, when everyone moves busily about. At this time (the start of things) one needs most composure, clarity, and concentration. A time of possibly tangled disputes. Be wary but pleasant.

Six in the second place: golden sunshine.
Supreme good fortune.
The midday sun, symbol of balance between the day's two halves. A time of harmony, success and recognition.

Nine in the third place: beneath the setting sun, old men beat on their pots and sing.
Others bemoan the approach of their last years. Misfortune.
Sadness and misfortune inevitably follow happiness and wealth. Faced with the painful reminders of change, some falsely 'escape' through gaiety, whilst others lament. Both extremes are foolish: only change is eternal. Only through calm acceptance can one keep one's virtue and continue to enjoy what one has. Trouble and dangers are indicated.

Nine in the fourth place: the sudden fire, which flares and dies, is forgotten.
The image of a 'flash' fire — arriving suddenly, powerfully and gone without useful result — serves as an analogy of the excitable entrepreneur, the Harry Hotspur, the passionate lover. Someone like this either consumes himself or the person on whom he feeds. He has little inner clarity. Do not waste resources, do not become excitable, do not be arrogant. Trouble accompanies such excesses.

Six in the fifth place: tears like a torrent.

Sighing, sadness. Auspicious.

A double meaning. The misplaced enthusiasms and excessive energies of one trying to change conditions leads to hurt and sorrow. Efforts will, nevertheless, be successful. The lamentations indicate a profound, sincere change of heart. In the context of the lines, this means a development towards a peaceful, virtuous nature. There is good fortune in this. A time of initial difficulty and even great upset — but the outcome will be good, later.

Nine at the top: he heads the royal forces, wisely killing the leaders, and capturing the followers. No blame.

There is virtue in achieving aims with the minimum of disruption. Likewise, things should be altered rather than destroyed, and people educated rather than coerced. An auspicious time, but one may be lonely, or alone.

▤ 31. HSIEN (*hr-syen*) /Stimulation

Below, Ken, the youngest son or young man (strength) has yielded to the upper trigram, Tui, the youngest daughter or young woman (the joyous). In a way fundamental to stable relationships, the man (the strong) yields to the woman, and the woman, likewise, yields to the man. This is the primary social contract with each partner subjugating his or her needs to that of the other. The image is persistent, quiet strength stimulating a weaker party, which responds joyously. Implied are affection, and sensitivity to others, or to externals — but not the so-called 'sensitivity' of the morbid introvert.

The Judgement

Stimulation: success.
Benefit in persevering.
Marriage to a girl is auspicious.

A successful, harmonious relationship is indicated. Because it is a proper and mutually caring union, success is sure to follow. This is true of any relationship — personal or formal.

The Image

The lake on the mountain, symbolizing Stimulation.
Thus the superior man encourages approach
By chivalrous demeanour.

The metaphor of a mountain lake suggests a receptive, calm character, rather than one who, knowing himself to be strong or superior, displays these qualities. The idea of unselfish principles is added to the notion of the strong willingly subordinating himself to the needs of the weak.

The Lines

Six at the bottom: stimulation of the big toe.

Predators wriggle before they spring; likewise, men about to fight often making a gripping motion with the big toe. The line indicates the intention to act, and a hasty, superficial approach. The situation may be more complex than one thinks, and one should wait patiently and observantly. Changes may be in the air, but do not over-react.

Six in the second place: stimulation in the calves.
Misfortune, unless you are still, then good fortune.

One is precipitous in action, or about to be so. The calves follow the feet — they are not self-governing. Thus one should wait until one has a strong principle, or very real condition upon which to base one's action. Remaining will bring a pleasant life.

Nine in the third place: stimulation in the thighs.
Following what it joins.
Regret if one continues.

A thoughtless action, automatic, like the movement of the

legs following that of the body, is indicated. The impulse should be resisted. The need for action is an illusion. Be cautious in behaviour.

Nine in the fourth place: benefit in persevering — guilt vanishes.
A man with agitated thoughts, his mind twitching, attracts only his closest.

Conflict is indicated between self and others, or between narrow considerations and inner truth. This promises no easy solutions. In quiet constancy, correctly executed, there is no regret. In conflict arising from the other path, one will be exhausted and ineffective.

Nine in the fifth place: stimulation in the upper back. No guilt.

The stiff upper back suggests the resolve of someone whose ideas come from deep conviction. This is accepted by those around you. Alternatively, one's apparent determination may be nothing more than stubbornness and sheer amorality. One should expect conflict.

Six at the top: stimulation in the mouth and tongue.
The 'stimulation' is talk, nothing more. With nothing behind it, nothing comes of it — no good, no bad.

☳☴ 32. HENG (*h'eng*)/Continuity

This hexagram is the inverse of that preceding: here Chen (eldest son, thunder) is above Sun (the eldest daughter, the gentle, wind). Thus the active leads the receptive and thunder joins wind (its natural companion) This suggests an enduring, consistent relationship.

The Judgement

Continuity. Success, no mistakes.

79

Persevering brings benefit.
Advancing towards objectives is beneficial.
Continuity is achieved through persistence, in the 'deep' sense. It is a quality of persevering at every instant, in the same, divinely creative sense that Vishnu, through his constant striding onwards, bridges the gaps between each moment, as they are destroyed by Shiva. This stresses the personal qualities of strength and wisdom which accompany the vital search for underlying meaning.

The Image

Thunder and wind, symbolizing Continuity.
Therefore, the superior man remains firm always,
Without straying from his path.
Although the two heavenly forces keep moving and change their change with little apparent continuity, they are in fact subject to the laws of life, like everything else. One should realize this and be utterly constant, although one might change one's tactics or behaviour to accommodate changing circumstances. In general, the harmony of the true continuity is stressed and distinguished from appearance.

The Lines

Six at the bottom: seeking continuity by grabbing brings only consistent misfortune. No benefit.
Only careful, sensitive and skilful effort can achieve enduring results. Hasty, unskilful, anxious endeavours attempt too much and fail. One should understand the nature of this time and reconcile oneself to it.

Nine in the second place: guilt vanishes.
By controlling excessive enthusiasm, grandiose ambitions, or improbable desires, one can achieve a stable position and avoid difficulties.

Nine in the third place: not maintaining continuity in his

character, he is disgraced, and has constant regret.
Inconsistent attitudes and lack of inner certainty bring
conflict with those around. Small, avoidable conflicts can
easily become major. Heed the advice of the Judgement
and Image.

Nine in the fourth place: no game in the preserve.
Just as there is no point in stalking game where none is
hiding, there is no point in persevering along the wrong
path. Try another approach. It is a time of frustration and
even some loss.

*Six in the fifth place: the continuity which comes from
perseverance.*
Auspicious for the wife; ominous for the husband.
A woman should be conservative while a man should
bend, but cling firmly to inner truth. Be consistent, but
avoid any artificiality or trickery.

Six at the top: the continuity of agitation. Misfortune.
Always hurrying hither and thither, one is always a few
minutes late, or a few steps ahead. Hurry and find a means
of regaining inner composure and tune into your
surroundings. No large undertakings now.

☰☶ 33. TUN (*t'hoon*)/Retreat

Ch'ien (older man, leader) above Ken (mountain, stillness)
suggests an isolated mountain hermit. Its emphasis is on
retreat from potentially harmful conditions, inspired by a
deep understanding of the results if one remains. Thus it
indicates retreat, isolation, or resignation underpinned by
acceptance of conditions as they are.

The Judgement

Retreat: success.
Persevering in small matters brings benefit.

The two weak lines indicate hostile forces in ascendancy. The wise person retreats — not running away, but giving way. Persevere, so that retreat is as constructive as possible.

The Image

The mountain reaching toward the sky symbolizes Retreat.
Superior men keep the lesser at a distance,
Not with anger, but with dignity.

The picture suggested is of the mountain, climbing towards heaven. Heaven appears to retreat upwards. In the same way, the wise keep a dignified distance between themselves and disturbing influences. The caution against negative feelings is particularly important.

The Lines

Six at the bottom: the tail retreating — dangerous.
One is content to undertake nothing.

The 'tail' is nearest the enemy, and in most danger. Difficulties are near. One should retreat quickly if necessary, otherwise remain peaceful and undertake nothing new.

Six in the second place: holding fast, bound with yellow oxhide.
No-one can tear him lose.

Yellow is the colour of the midday sun — of the midpoint and of balance. Oxhide is almost unbreakable, so the image represents someone clinging to another of superior virtue or strength, or to unshakable principles. Without specific comment, the line is favourable. Calmness and imperturbability are favoured.

Nine in the third place: an entangled retreat is dangerous and distressing.
Benevolence towards one's servants. Auspicious.

Complications during retreat which prove frustrating and dangerous. Compromise is necessary with the hindering force, so that one may retain some freedom of action. One cannot count on help now, though it may come unexpectedly.

Nine in the fourth place: voluntary retreat.
Auspicious for the superior man, dangerous for the inferior.
A time of little opportunity, except to withdraw completely to avoid downfall. Graceful withdrawal entails no loss of honour whilst that accomplished with regret causes damage all round and inestimable psychic harm.

Nine in the fifth place: retreat with sensibility.
Persevering is auspicious.
Choose the moment for retreat carefully, so all occurs in a smooth and friendly manner. In this way one attracts others of similar outlook, and avoids severing existing links completely. One may receive help or even promotion now.

Nine at the top: retreat with happy demeanour.
Benefit in every place.
The state of mind of one utterly equable about retreat is indicated here. The way ahead is clear in one's mind and benefits naturally accrue from this certainty. A time of withdrawal if it seems appropriate, of waiting if one is about to start undertakings, and of success in established enterprises.

34. TA CHUANG (*da zhw'ng*) /Great Power

The trigram Chen, above Ch'ien (heaven) shows thunder in the heavens. The attributes of a young man (strength, movement) add to the naturalistic image of young, vital power. In one way Ta Chuang is the opposite of Tun, where the dark, hostile forces were ascending. Here, strong, creative forces move upwards. When conditions are favourable, results will be excellent, but there is always great danger of excess and misuse of power.

The Judgement

Great Power: perseverance brings benefit.
The image of Great Power is self-explanatory, but the authors have added the most important qualification. This is that Great Power should be tempered either by perseverance in restricting and restraining oneself in accordance with what is right, or by persevering in waiting for the right time. Whichever applies, the marriage of power and sensitivity is vital to produce good, fruitful results, rather than waste.

The Image

Thunder in the high heavens, symbolizing Great Power.
Therefore, the superior man does not conduct himself
In opposition to the established order.
Thunder is moving towards heaven. Both have upward tendencies, so their movements are in harmony. This happy tendency must be guarded by doing nothing incompatible with the correct way — whether the way is the law, efficiency or the simple voice within.

The Lines

Nine at the bottom: power in the toes.
Advance brings misfortune. This is certain.
The toes or the lowliest part — significant advance should not be prompted merely by tapping toes! Impulse and reckless prompting should be firmly resisted. A time of conflicts, regret, unpopularity and peril.

Nine in the second place: perseverance is fortunate.
Resistance is beginning to fade, success seems likely. Act

properly, maintain and develop inner calm. In this way you will succeed.

Nine in the third place: the inferior man uses his strength, the superior man does not.
The goat charges a thorn bush and is trapped by the horns.
Advance is perilous.

One uses force; the other uses skill. This is the warning against the abuse of power. There is another abuse, that is, to shrink from power. It must be understood and made fully part of oneself. This has natural, beneficial influence. Beware conflicts which may entangle you.

Nine in the fourth place: persevering brings good fortune, guilt vanishes.
The thornbush gives way without catching.
Power like the spokes under the big wagon.

Obstacles vanish: success. The power accomplishing this is like the spokes of a wagon wheel which are individually insignificant, but which radiate in all directions applying their influence evenly in every area like a thorough, well-balanced man. A time when activity begins again and advancement is likely.

Six in the fifth place: taking his ease, he loses the goat. No guilt.

Mellowing influences have removed the stubborn, aggressive, narrow quality. However, this line indicates inner weakness and this is not auspicious for undertakings or for anyone hoping for recognition.

Six at the top: the goat charges the thorn bush, and is stuck fast.
There is no improvement in any place.
Acceptance is auspicious.

This is the line of illusion, arrogance and subbornness, and its fruition is deadlock, conflict and even hatred. Only complete acceptance can avoid this.

35. CHIN (*tzchin*)/Progress

The sun (Li) is above the earth (K'un) at the beginning of the day, symbolizing increasing influence, easy progress and prosperity. In human terms, there are two parties represented: one active, passionate and forward-looking; the other passive, receptive and logical. Warnings here concern the possibility of separation (the sun 'leaves' the earth), undue haste (the sun's progress is the basic symbol of regulated, proper development) and of incorrect relationships.

The Judgement

Progress. The powerful, rich, respected noble
Is honoured with gifts of many horses.
The king receives him thrice in a single day.

This shows an earthly relationship corresponding to the correctness within the natural symbolism. Respected by his peers, the leader is dutiful and correct toward his king, who honours him. Thus the idea of an independent, but obedient servant, and a just, understanding master, is presented as the foundation of progress in great matters.

The Image

The sun rising over the earth symbolizes progress.
Thus the superior man brightens his virtue.

The early sun brightens as it rises, leaving the dark below. Thus the wise improve their position and character by discarding the shabby and the unprincipled. In this way they gain in self-reliance and virtue.

The Lines

Six at the bottom: progress obstructed.
Persevering is auspicious.

*One unable to inspire others should accept this with
 equanimity.*
Others may have no confidence in us and equally, we may
lack confidence. The way onward lies in calm persistence.

*Six in the second place: progressing sorrowfully,
 perseverance is auspicious.*
*Graciousness in great part from one's mother's mother, in
 spirit.*
The source of your status, or power, or the one on whom
you depend, is barred to you. If the relationship between
you is solid and correct, the other may soften towards you.
Alternatively, one's own persistence, softened by sadness,
may open another way to you. A time of difficulty followed
by harmony.

*Six in the third place: the people trust him and there is no
 guilt.*
All are in accord, and this common will and energy
removes any doubts about one's own, individual
shortcomings. A time of possible loss, but also of possible
advancement.

*Nine in the fourth place: progressing like a hamster, there is
 danger in persevering.*
Scurrying hither and thither, secretively storing up one's
treasures, alienates others and will invariably be scorned as
conditions expose one's behaviour. This is not the time to
advance. Generally, conflict is likely.

Six in the fifth place: remorse vanishes.
Do not heed gain or loss.
Advance is auspicious; in every place, benefit.
In an influential, creative position, one must remain
reserved. Regret is foolish; similarly, one should realize that
the real position is excellent and progressing. A time of
advancement.

Nine at the top: progressing with lowered horns — only for

chastising his own city.
Awareness of dangerous circumstances is auspicious,
  without harm.
Perseverance brings regret.
Normally friendly relationships are ordered according to
mutual principles, and acquiescence ensures harmony. But
this is one time when firm, even punitive action is needed
to restore correct conditions or stop the rot. But do not
employ aggression where none is needed.

☷☲ 36. MIN I (*mingy'ee*) /Darkening of the Light

Here the trigrams position is the opposite of Chin. Here
K'un, the earth, is above Li, the sun or light. Hence the
image of approaching nightfall, or the darkening of the
light. Implications include the crushing accumulation of
hostile or negative (weak) forces, and the omnipotence of
an authority inimical to one's beliefs. In relationships, one
may find things sad and grotesque, whilst everyone else
seems blithely unaware of these (to you) hateful conditions.

The Judgement

Darkening of the light.
Adversity means benefit must accrue through persevering.
Activity brings wounds for the initiator, and little, if any,
successes. One should 'hide one's light under a bushel', if
one's light is producing any useful brilliance. If it is not, one
should work constantly at improving one's virtue. Thus one
learns invaluable lessons from this time, and is prepared
when a favourable time for action comes.

The Image

The sun sinking below the earth symbolizes Darkening of

the Light.
*In this way the superior man remains in harmony with the
people;*
Hiding his brilliance, whilst his virtue still shines.

The wise person is now cautious, reserved and considerate.
when surrounding forces are hostile, as indicated by Ming I,
one should not invite open emnity by immodest behaviour.

The Lines

*Nine at the bottom: darkened light flies, with drooping
wings.*
*The superior man fasts for three days during his
wanderings.*
But he has a destination.
His host derides him.

The picture of this line is of one who attempts to avoid
danger by ignoring it. A time of mixed fortunes. Grandiose
intentions are unsuccessful, so one retreats. Then one must
carry on with greater resolve, despite hardships and the fact
that one will earn only derision from those around (even
those closest).

Sticking to one's principles may bring further hardship,
though it is not necessarily inappropriate at this time. There
is a likelihood of promotion and reward for some, but
those in difficulties should withdraw.

*Six in the second place: darkening of the light injures his
left thigh.*
A strong horse assists him in salvation. Auspicious.

Two meanings are suggested, either the subject is injured
and receives help, or he gives help to others similarly
afflicted. Generally, the situation is still reversible with the
help of like-minded people. A time of promotion.

*Nine in the third place: darkening of the light over the
hunting party in the south.*
The leader is captured.

Do not try to rectify all abuses immediately.
One has ignored the prevailing signs and continues, injuring a 'figurehead'. One can expect real trouble to rebound. Or, one is able to 'capture' the source of the difficulty and neutralize it or him. but one must not expect to set conditions right for a long time. A time of travel or conflict.

Six in the fourth place: entering the belly of the dark through the left side.
He wins the heart of the dark: he slips out by the gate.
Able to understand the hostile forces one realizes how serious the danger is, although one can withdraw without trouble. A time of help from others, but there are also troubles.

Six in the fifth place: the darkened light of Prince Chi.
Persevere in your course.
The Prince was a Hamlet-like figure, bound by family honour to the court of a corrupt and evil king. Thus he feigned madness and so escaped undue involvement with the evil around him. The moral is to restrain oneself and remain active but accepting.

Six at the top: no light, but obscurity.
First he ascended to heaven; then he descends to the bowels of the earth.
The dark force has reached its extreme and collapses. It may have left one numbed, but now suffering is at an end. Beware of losing what is established, or of difficulties after advance.

≡ 37. CHIA JEN (*kjhee-ah rzh'n*)/The Family

The structure of a family is indicated in the lines. Members indicated by yin or yang lines correlate with the correct partner in the hexagram, so the emphasis is on correct relationships, co-operation, responsibilities and harmonious, conscientious attitudes.

The Judgement

The Family. There is benefit in womanly perseverance.

If the correct attitudes prevail, the family structure will remain strong and contribute to a harmonious society. The basic union is that of man and wife. It is her devotion and persevering loyalty which holds this together. The woman is, therefore, the foundation of marriage and society.

The Image

Wind blowing out of fire symbolizes the Family.
Thus the speech of the superior man should have substance,
And the style of his life be enduring.

The man is the outward strength of the family. Like a flame which needs fuel, his words must be based on substance: like blowing a sail, his conduct must support his words to give them effectiveness.

The Lines

Nine at the bottom: he makes the rules for his family.
Regret vanishes.

When one begins activity with definite responsibilities and authority, it is vital to exercise power firmly and correctly at the beginning. This may cause trouble at first, but only in this way can a proper status quo be set up. Then unhappiness vanishes. A time of promotion, advance and recognition.

Six in the second place: she must attend to her duties, and cook the food.
Perseverance is auspicious.

A time of improvement and success. One should attend to one's responsibilities as the social and spiritual linchpin of one's environment. Quiet, correct perseverance is stressed.

*Nine in the third place: in family disputes, too much
sternness is later regretted.*
Chattering women and children bring humiliation.
Auspicious, with danger.

The father's correction should be firm, not excessive —
although it is better to be too hard than too soft. If one
now has the choice between a free environment and a
limited setting, choose restraint. A time of tendency
towards bad habits.

*Six in the fourth place: she enriches the family. Greatly
auspicious.*

Prosperity and recognition is indicated. The woman was
the steward of the household, dealing skilfully and
harmoniously with material responsibilities. This is a model
for one in the position of a custodian or steward.

*Nine in the fifth place: the king extends his influence to his
whole family.*
No anxieties. Good fortune.

The father should govern his family like a king, through
love and virtue. Such a man, in a wider sphere, has the
respect and confidence of all. A time of benefit through
others' help.

Nine at the top: his sincerity is honoured.
Good fortune in the end.

A time of recognition, reward and general success is
indicated. In society, the good order of a family depends on
its head. He must recognize his responsibilities and
influence, and live up to them.

▤ 38. K'UEI (*khwei*) /Neutrality and Disunity

Li (the flame) and Tui (the lake, below) have no interaction:

the tendency of flame is upward, that of water, down. Thus the current condition is one of a disunity. This may mean actual or latent conflict.

The Judgement

Disunity. In minor patterns, success.
The situation may appear weighty and stagnant, with no creative union, but a larger or broader view shows that it contains opposing elements which can, together, be creative. This may be external or within oneself. But there are practical obstacles and so only minor achievements are possible.

The Image

Fire above the lake symbolizes Neutrality.
Thus, in the midst of the many,
The superior man understands individuality.
Fire and water always retain their own nature, however close their association. Similarly, a wise person should not be affected by the prevailing moods, but should first rely on his own standards. This also indicates how one might change for the better. When one is isolated or in conflict with things or people, one should become more generous towards others, whilst retaining one's own individuality.

The Lines

Nine at the bottom: if you lose your horse, do not follow.
It will return by itself.
If you meet evil men, guard your conduct. Guilt disappears.
Do not try to recover what is lost: it will return only if it is proper for it to do so. One should simply endure bad conditions and people now, guarding against thoughtless mistakes whilst remaining neutral. A time of temporary setbacks followed by progress.

Nine in the second place: he meets his lord in a back alley.
No mistakes.

The normal affinity between people is missing, due to misunderstanding. Perhaps a compromise is called for or, more literally, an 'accidental' meeting. Success through others is indicated.

Six in the third place: he sees the cart halted, the ox team
    dragged to a stop.
The man's hair and nose are cut off.
A bad start but a good end.

A time of complicated, dangerous obstacles, followed by harmony. One feels as though everything is going wrong. Hold fast to what is right and good fortune will soon equal misfortune.

Nine in the fourth place: isolation through conflict, he
    meets a strong man of the same goodwill.
Danger continues, but there is no mistake.

Even when isolated by one's antipathy one can avoid the perils of loneliness with the help of an empathetic partner. There may be limitations in such a relationship. A time of help from others, safety in the midst of danger and harmony after trouble.

Six in the fifth place: he uses his teeth to cling to a relation.
How could there be mistakes if one goes along, with such
    help?

A time of alienation, then the revealing of a kindred spirit. Joining forces with this figure would be beneficial if the relationship was sincere.

Nine at the top: isolated through conflict, he sees them, a
    pig covered with filth, devils in a cart.
He draws his bow; lays it down.
He is not an assailant: he will become a suitor.
Advance and soft rain. Good fortune.

Mistakenly believing an approach is aggressive, self-seeking, or cold-hearted, one is mistrustful. Acceptance is necessary, and it will become obvious after the tension has cleared, that all is well. Troubles will clear, assisted by a correct attitude.

39. CHIEN (*khy'n*) /Obstruction

The hexagram means difficulty, danger or obstruction. K'an (water) is above Ken (the mountain) representing a temporary lake which may be released and crash down on the villages and crops below. The image of an abyss (K'an) ahead, with the mountain behind, indicates the danger or difficulty of movement.

The Judgement

> *Obstruction. The south-west is of benefit.*
> *The north-east is of no benefit.*
> *There is benefit in visiting the great man.*
> *Persevering is auspicious.*

The south-west is linked with the trigram K'un (the plain) where the dangerous force of water would be quietened to the benefit of the community. The leadership of a higher authority — whether it is a living person, a set of rules or an ideal — may be necessary to escape. Concentrate on maintaining a harmonious attitude and do not be pressurized into adopting conventional, ultimately useless 'solutions'.

The Image

> *Water on the mountain symbolizes Obstruction.*
> *The superior man directs his attention inwards*
> *And cultivates his virtue.*

The unpleasantness we experience when in difficulty is, more often than not, caused by our own reactions. One should not try to 'work things out' neurotically and uselessly, but develop both sensitivity to one's condition and an attitude which creates harmony.

The Lines

Six at the bottom: advance brings obstructions.
Retreat brings praise.

Pressing on now is a yang, hard path. If one can do this, so be it. Staying is yin — soft and not difficult. It is a question of what is realistic. This is a time of neutral fortune, and not one for undertaking anything new.

Six in the second place: the king's messenger encounters many obstacles.
No fault of his.

Beset with difficulties — real or illusory — one would normally withdraw. But a definite commitment is indicated and one can, and must, accept it.

Nine in the third place: advance brings obstructions.
Therefore he retreats.

Whether one wishes to go ahead or not, others' dependence means we may not do so. This line advises caution and suggests favourable unions or promotion.

Six in the fourth place: advance brings obstructions.
Retreat means harmonious alliances.

There is great danger of taking support for granted, miscalculating one's strengths and plunging into trouble. Better to hold back, make certain of support, and wait for a favourable time. Be diligent, cautious and humble now. This will be fortunate.

Nine in the fifth place: he struggles with terrible difficulties.
Friends come to his aid.

One may be faced with a serious situation which requires action, though the problems seem insurmountable. But a responsible spirit will attract others. Alternatively, one may take on another's problem for them. All will be well. Help and good fortune for oneself are indicated.

> *Six at the top: advance brings obstructions, retreat brings auspicious conditions.*
> *Benefit in visiting the great man.*

One would like nothing more than to leave the mess alone: it seems petty and unpleasant. But trouble and values seem to draw you back. Face these problems with an elightened, unselfish attitude — on this rests the auspicious nature of the judgement. Seek the help of authority, strength or wisdom. A time of progress and recognition.

☷☵ 40. HSIEH (*khee-eh*) /Liberation

This hexagram represents a release from the worries of Chien. The time indicated is spring, or early morning: both mean new life and opportunities for hard work. The signs of imminent salvation or success bring the danger of relaxing prematurely and also of taking up any activity interrupted by the past troubles. Look forward.

The Judgement

> *Liberation. The south-west is of benefit.*
> *If nothing remains to be done,*
> *Returning is correct.*
> *If something remains to be done,*
> *Haste is correct.*

Conditions are tending to return to normal (the south-west, symbolizes a plain, where there is conventional human activity) and things should be arranged in the proper way as soon as possible. Be careful of over-enthusiasm or excess. One should remain on guard, so that one is free to carry on with the new time.

The Image

Rolling thunder, followed by rain, symbolizes Liberation.
Thus the superior man forgives errors
And deals compassionately with wrong-doing.

Release from tension follows thunder-storms: similarly, forgiveness for mistakes and misdeeds clears the situation. This is the hexagram symbolizing the Zen Buddhist's koan, or the kumite experience in martial arts — both embody mental anguish and confusion, followed by subtle, intense clarity. This is the clarity one should have just prior to a great undertaking.

The Lines

Six at the bottom: no blame.

One has done well to endure past difficulties, now there is peace. If starting projects or facing challenges, this line indicates success.

Nine in the second place: he kills three foxes in the hunt.
He obtains golden arrows.
Good fortune if the man perseveres.

Foxes symbolize cunning or insincere people; yellow (the colour of the average or correctness) with the image of the arrows (which fly straight), together symbolize directness and measured action. The image is of a man's natural skill or service gaining him a position which requires less spontaneity and more consideration. A time of promotion and gain.

Six in the third place: with his goods in a sling on his back,
Nevertheless, transported in a carriage, he invites robbery.
Continuing in this way means regret.

Escaping from hard circumstances carries the burden of the past. He may begin to assume airs and graces, or relax unduly. Be careful and correct, despite apparently good times.

Nine in the fourth place: let go of your big toe.
When your friend arrives, you may trust him.

The big toe symbolizes an untrustworthy inferior person who has become attached to the superior. One must relinquish the bad influence or lose the better fortune which lies in the future.

Six in the fifth place: liberating himself brings good fortune
  to the superior man.
Thus he has the confidence of the inferior.

Liberation, in whatever sense, requires effort. this is vital. A time of inner resolve, significant actions and, with correct attitudes, success.

Six at the top: the prince shoots a hawk on the high wall,
  hitting it.
Benefit in every place.

The hawk symbolizes a bad attitude or inferior person that has acquired unwarranted importance and must be quickly removed. The technique is vital and one should consider carefully before acting. A time of promotion, recognition, and success.

☶ 41. SUN (*suin*)/Decrease

Decrease, even loss, is symbolized by Ken, the mountain, above Tui, the lake — the mountain's edge crumbling into the water. But whilst one part is reduced, the other is increased. One man's loss is another man's gain. The theme of Sun concerns adjustment to this time.

The Judgement

Decrease; with sincerity.
There is great good fortune, without mistakes.
You may continue.
Advancing is beneficial.

How should one advance?
By the sacrifice of two bowls of rice.

Understanding the inevitability of the time is of vital and fundamental importance. Austerity, simplicity and humility are right and proper. With this simple understanding, one can achieve a great deal. The sacrifice of two bowls of rice — like the story of the widow's mite (Gospel according to St Luke) — indicates that even the smallest actions, if sincere, can be good.

The Image

The lake lapping at the foot of the mountain symbolizes Decrease.
Thus the superior man curbs his anger.
And controls his desires.

The mountain, symbolizing stubbornness, hardness, even anger, crumbles into the lake of joy and happiness. The dissolving of hardness brings joy. Hysterical gaiety and silliness are avoided as the lake evaporates, giving beneficial moisture to the mountain slopes. There is no advantage in sadness. One may lose friends, find share dividends decreasing but by readjusting one's values one can improve one's character inestimably.

The Lines

Nine at the bottom: going quickly when the work is done, is without blame.
But consider carefully what the decrease will be.

The line symbolizes one helping another, because he is unable to carry on his own business. However, both sides could suffer if the helper is giving too much of himself, or if his aid is an intrusion. A time when one might expect to help othes, and gain others' approval.

Nine in the second place: perseverance is beneficial, but

advancing is ominous.
One can benefit others without decreasing oneself.

A time when advance is unlikely and forward planning is ill-advised. The line indicates one prevailed upon to assist in something that goes against the grain, or is likely to impose a stress. Retain one's integrity, first and foremost, because once this is lost one is of no use to self or others.

Six in the third place: three people walk together and lose one.
One walking alone finds friendship.

Three form an impossible triangle: one must go. But that person will find another relationship. A time of help from others.

Six in the fourth place: if he reduces his faults, another soon rejoices.
No mistakes here.

A time when people are eager to help, without obligation, and when bad times seem to vanish.

Six in the fifth place: he is greatly enriched,
Ten pairs of tortoises cannot oppose this.
Supremely auspicious.

A time of natural good luck. Any oracle — represented by the tortoises whose shells were used in the ancient Chinese method — would say so.

Nine at the top: in personal increase without decrease for others, there is no blame.
Persevering is auspicious.
Benefit in advancing.
One finds helpers from every clan after leaving home.

One who is supremely successful, without exploiting others, is indicated. Success comes from unselfishness, so it is shared. His virtue assures help wherever he goes. Recognition, respect and general success are indicated.

☴ 42. I (*yee*)/Increase

I suggests a luxuriant forest, full of blooming flowers and plants (produced by Sun, above and Chen, the arousing force, below). Also, the bottom line of the upper trigram is thought to have yielded to make way for a yin or weak line. This suggests consideration and service by the strong. Such self-effacement is considered supremely auspicious.

The Judgement

Increase. Benefit in setting forth.
Benefit in crossing the great water.

The time of increase will not last, therefore now is the time to act, without hesitating. This applies even to major, dangerous enterprises.

The Image

Wind and thunder complementing each other symbolize Increase.
Thus the superior man observes good, and follows it;
Observes what is faulty, and corrects it.

I has a dual aspect; but while the stress of Sun is on decrease, here it is on gain and progress. One should not take good fortune for granted. The imagery may apply to relationships, where one partner believes himself to be generous, but is in fact feeding egotistically on the other's selfless support. The need is indicated for awareness and self-examination.

The Lines

Nine at the bottom: benefit in great undertakings.
Supremely auspicious; no mistakes here.

Without guilt at one's enormous good fortune, perhaps at the apparent expense of others, one must use this time to achieve. Beware of selfishness. A time of tremendous success.

Six in the second place: he is greatly enriched.
Ten pairs of tortoises cannot oppose this.
Continuing, persevering is auspicious.
The king honours him at the altar of the Absolute. Good
   fortune.

Some opposition to the help or fortune which is due is indicated. But, as any oracle (ten pairs of tortoise shells) would testify, fortune is on one's side. The image of honour before the highest principle stresses that success is the result of one's inward love of good.

Six in the third place: increase by unfortunate conditions.
No guilt attends this, if one is sincere, follows the middle
   way, and is like one who carries the official seal.

A time of success and new responsibilities. A generous gesture or aid results in rewards. Wise people are in harmony with the times and their actions have a natural authority.

Six in the fourth place: if he keeps to the middle way, even
   the prince will follow his counsel.
Benefit in trustworthiness, even in re-establishing the
   capital.

One who is trusted should never take advantage of this position. When a major undertaking is called for, he should shoulder the responsibility in accord with the needs of the time. A time of moving, fresh responsibilities and successful opportunities.

Nine in the fifth place: kind sincerity does not make
   demands.
Supremely auspicious.
Without doubt, people trust such kindness.

Sincere kindness does not expect reward or tot up merit. A time of self-improvement, promotion, more responsibilities and successful opportunities.

Nine at the top: increase to no one, someone beats him.
His heart is inconstant. Ominous.

A time of dislike, insults, retribution and loss. Someone who has neglected his duty to share his good fortune becomes alienated, isolated and despised. One's principles may be good, but one's actions do not reflect the spirit within. This line advises a concentrated and, above all, a calm, reflective attitude.

▆▆ 43. KUAI (*gwie*) /Determination

This hexagram indicates a decision, or breakthrough after a long period of tension, symbolized by an imminent cloudburst (Tui, the lake, above Ch'ien, heaven) or a time when the inferior begin to lose ground. Its theme is the force which can equally create great good or cause unpleasantness and disharmony everywhere. The advice of Kuai is on how this energy should be channelled.

The Judgement

Determination. The matter must be exposed in the highest
*   courts,*
Resolutely and earnestly.
Danger, then.
It must be announced to one's people,
But no force should benefit now.
Benefit in advancing.

The smallest faults should be corrected. This requires firmness and determination. One should be honest and open, though it might seem strategically unwise. Any kind of help should be seriously considered, but one should not fight fire with fire. The hostile force is now at a low point.

The Image

The lake risen to overflowing, to heaven: the symbol of

Determination.
Thus the superior man distributes wealth below him
And does not allow his gifts to remain unused.

A situation is shown where conditions, or a person, are strong and influential. Things will change. Good or bad results depend on the attitude of the central figure, and of others' feelings toward him. All gain is followed by loss, so the wise person shares his wealth, and does not allow himself to become isolated by ignoring life around him.

The Lines

Nine at the bottom: power in the advancing toes.
Moving forward without ability, mistakes and no
improvements.

If one is unequal to the task ahead, tackling it will bring nothing but trouble. A time of conflict caused by immodesty.

Nine in the second place: he cries out in alarm.
Taking arms against the unexpected.
Steady, without fear.

Determination requires sensitivity and caution. Expect the unexpected: a time of danger is indicated. But quiet, working people may get benefit. The lesson of the line is that reason should triumph over passion.

Nine in the third place: showing force in one's face is
ominous.
The superior man is determined and walks alone through
the rain.
He is caught in the flood; he is hated. No blame, in the end.

A time of unpleasantness with others. However, by firmly maintaining correct attitudes and behaviour, there will be good fortune.

Nine in the fourth place: with the skin flayed from his
thighs, he may hardly walk.
Were he to be sheep-like, following, shame would disappear.

But he is deaf to these words.

One is restless and assertive, too obstinate to understand the nature of the obstacles ahead. Only by heeding advice, acting sensitively and by moving delicately could one benefit — but one is deafened by obstinancy.

Nine in the fifth place: clearing weeds requires constant firmness.
The middle way is without mistake.

The struggle against evil never ends and one must always realize its existence. But we must accept the presence of the bad without becoming too familiar with it. Remain principled and resolute. The Middle Way of Buddhism is the ideal and one should only cultivate what is good. When the bad is purged one should be careful not to destroy the good with it. A time of achievement after difficulties.

Six at the top: no call for help. Ominous in the end.

New projects are ill-advised. Conflicts, bitterness and family complications are also indicated here. The lesson of the line is that when aims seem to have been achieved, destructive forces can break out and destroy everything. One must be vitally aware of this.

☰ 44. KOU (*gaou*)/Tempting Encounter

The weak principle intrudes, indicating the appearance of a dangerous, though apparently harmless element. Above, Ch'ien, a strong force, meets Sun, a feminine and penetrating force. This suggests a male principle — a leader, an authoritative person or a stable, strong situation — influenced by a weak but effective element. Kou is favourable for short-term projects.

The Judgement

Tempting Encounter.

The girl is forceful.
One should not marry her.
The weak element attracts attention. In this way inferior people rise to positions of power. If there is no deceit, and no ulterior motive, the situation can be truly happy — but this requires profound insight and virtue.

The Image

Wind blowing under heaven, symbolizing Tempting
Encounter.
The prince thus issues his pronouncements,
Proclaiming them to the farthest corners of the world.
Here the wind disseminates the creative influence. Organization and great activity is suggested. The implicit warning is against lacking humility and sensitivity to the changing forces which surround one.

The Lines

Six at the bottom: he must be controlled as if with a metal
brake.
Perseverance is auspicious.
Advancing is ominous.
Even a small pig's raging is destructive.
An inferior element creeping in, an unchecked desire — both should be checked immediately before they cause damage. The control must continue. No advance, though it may be fruitful for quiet types.

Nine in the second place: fish in a container.
No blame, no benefit for the guest.
One should keep an inferior or dangerous element under control, and not allow it to come in contact with those one loves or respects. A time of assistance and promotion.

Nine in the third place: with the skin flayed from his thighs,
he can hardly walk.

No great harm in this, with awareness of danger.
There is danger of being influenced by weak principles, or inferior elements now, but something prevents it. Insight would help one escape danger. Misfortune is indicated, though people with quiet life-styles may be fortunate.

Nine in the fourth place: no fish in the container. Bad fortune.
One has been seduced by inferior elements which now withdraw. Perhaps one should tolerate seeming inferiors in order to avoid alienating them. Conflict and slander is indicated.

Nine in the fifth place: a melon lying beneath the foliage of a tree.
Splendour concealed. Blessing from heaven.
The image is of a tempting fruit which spoils easily. It is protected by leaves. Thus a wise person tolerates and cares for inferior, weak elements and does not bother others with displays of virtue. One can receive benefit from soft people (or the 'softness' of pleasure) by consistent, firm — but not overbearing or critical — behaviour. A time of help and recognition is indicated.

Nine at the top: encounter with horns lowered.
Regret, but no mistakes.
A situation where one has withdrawn from inferior or bad elements but one is brusque, perhaps violent, and consequently despised. Understand, therefore, the need for composure. A time of difficulty, but with greater responsibility, is indicated.

☱☷ 45. TS'UI (*tzhweay*)/In Accord

The image suggested by Tui (a lake), above K'un (the earth) is of water collecting into a single mass (in contrast with Pi, the eighth hexagram, which represents a more stable condition). This suggests people gathering together in accord. The implicit warning is against disorder. It is a time to establish stable, ordered durable conditions.

The Judgement

In accord. Success.
The king goes to the temple.
Seeing the great man brings success.
Perseverance is beneficial.
Making offerings creates good fortune.
Benefit in undertaking.

Communities achieve prosperity by acting in accord. Here, emphasis is put upon the leader — the king. The advantages of agreement are increased by the offerings which each leader makes. The needs of the group are, or should be, underlying one's attitudes. However, the deep meaning of Ts'ui deals with the 'centre' — that is, not necessarily the person who appears to be the leader, but the guiding, coherent force which underlies any fruitful association.

The Image

The lake gathered on the earth, symbolizing In Accord.
Thus the superior man has weapons ready
To deal with the unexpected.

At this time, symbolized by a lake held in the embrace of the earth, there is always the possibility that the water will overflow — bringing sudden danger. This could come either from the group (even though harmony apparently prevails), or from outside.

The Lines

Six at the bottom: sincerity, but without completion, brings
*   accord, then confusion.*
First crying out, he shakes a hand, then can smile with
*   happiness.*

Do not worry: there is no mistake.

There is a real need for a leader. A suitable person — already the centre of strength and purpose — exists, and he should be approached. The group must recognize their need and its solution. A time of difficulty, then good fortune.

> *Six in the second place: being drawn into accord brings good fortune. No guilt.*
> *If one is sincere, even a small offering is beneficial.*

Without doubt there is an inner force which attracts one to a certain path. This is not arbitrary at all, but correct and fortunate. Just as a humble offering is appreciated by sincere, sensitive people, one's choice will be complemented by the subtle compatibility of the path our inner voice dictates. A time of help and promotion.

> *Six in the third place: accordance, with much sighing.*
> *No benefit in undertakings; no worth in advance.*
> *No great mistake in undertaking, but some regret.*

One feels isolated and humiliated. Only resolute progress toward the centre can achieve anything, though it will not be easy. One should be cautious. Difficulties, then relief are indicated.

> *Nine in the fourth place: supremely auspicious. No blame.*

One who is a valued and respected group member is indicated. His success is unselfish, he works on behalf of others and shares their good fortune or sadness. A time of trouble through incorrect conduct or disputes. Even hatred is suggested.

> *Nine in the fifth place: if one who is in accord with others has status, there is no blame.*
> *If some doubt the cause, great and consistent perseverance is necessary.*
> *Then guilt will vanish.*

When people gather around, it is gratifying and perhaps useful — unless the attraction is only superficial status.

One should be open and principled in dealing with them. Deal directly with any mistrust or doubt. Disharmony and difficulties are indicated.

Six at the top: wailing and weeping, but no mistakes.
It is impossible to be in accord and one laments. This is natural and timely. A time of sadness and unsettled conditions are likely.

46. SHENG (*sh'ng*)/Pushing Upward

The time indicated here is spring: below, plants (symbolized by Sun, wood) push upward through the earth (K'un), suggesting expansion and growth. The emphasis is on upward motion (from obscurity to influence, for instance) rather than simple expansion. Willpower and control are necessary to order this movement harmoniously.

The Judgement

Pushing Upward. Supreme success.
One should see the great man: no fear.
Advance to the south brings good fortune.
One should be careful and correct in one's attitudes, or selfishness may take over and lead to misfortune. Carried along by good fortune, one should seek the advice of an authoritative person. The south symbolizes activity. Unselfish application will now create lasting harmony. A favourable time to establish lasting conditions.

The Image

Wood growing in the earth symbolizes Pushing Upward.
The superior man devotes himself to building up, piece by piece,
From small beginnings to great achievements.

Constant, flexible growth is the attribute of a plant pushing upwards. A wise person, in harmony with fate, is sensitive and determined.

The Lines

Six at the bottom: confident pushing upward. Greatly auspicious.

Even though one's position is now insignificant, one's efforts will win approval. Success far beyond expectation is possible.

Nine in the second place: if he is sincere, the smallest offering is beneficial. No mistakes.

The subject has limited resources but his efforts are nevertheless appreciated. Alternatively, a robust character is indicated, whose inner soundness compensates for his outward lack of style. A time of advance, although sadness is also implied.

Nine in the third place: he climbs up to the deserted city.

The image to one who either finds an easy path opening up or who chooses the line of least resistance. He achieves his goal, but the commentary has no suggestion of lasting good fortune. This may be superficially auspicious.

Six in the fourth place: the king offers a place on Mount Ch'i.

Auspicious, no mistakes.

King Wen offered the most honoured a niche in the great mountain temple of Ch'i. The line suggests reaching a goal and attaining special influence. Travel is favoured.

Six in the fifth place: perseverance in pushing upward is auspicious.

Benefit in advancing consistently.

As one progresses and as success appears closer, carelessness and short cuts are easy mistakes. Remember, success will only be achieved through untiring and correct effort.

Six at the top: pushing blindly upward.
It is beneficial to persevere without relaxing.

Always forging ahead is the mark of blind ambition. Only consistent, conscious effort can sustain such unnatural progress.

47. K'UN (*khw'n*) /Oppression

This is one of the major 'danger signs' of the *I Ching*, signifying extreme difficulty, poverty and oppression. Exhaustion is symbolized by K'an (water) lying under Tui (the lake). The lake is empty and its water drained away. The lines — one weak holding down two strong and two weak enclosing one strong — suggest restriction, obstacles and oppression. All six lines are unfavourable, but the most extreme misfortune bears the seeds of great regeneration, if one can understand and absorb the hard spirit of the time.

The Judgement

Oppression. Success. Perseverance.
Good fortune attends the great man. No mistake, then.
What is stated with words is not believed.

Adversity can make or break us. If we do not learn from adverse conditions we will be broken. It requires greatness to learn from bad times whilst cultivating inner virtue. Outward virtue will have no effect. It is a time to develop the character unceasingly but to display it with modesty.

The Image

The lake without water symbolizes Oppression.
The superior man knows his life depends
On persevering in his Way.

Ensnared and disillusioned, one finds oneself at a crisis

113

point when the facile dreams and corrupt principles are found to be empty. One's attitudes and actions will steer one's life for years to come. There is nothing more vital now than to acquiesce to the nature of one's condition and to understanding one's own spirit.

The Lines

Six at the bottom: oppressed beneath a withered tree, he stared into a dark valley.
He sees nothing for three years.

One is overcome by the illusion that difficulties are too strong. However grim things seem, these delusions must be overcome.

Nine in the second place: oppressed, though he eats and drinks.
The figure with scarlet trappings approaches.
Benefit in sacrifice.
Misfortune in initiative, but no blame.

Outwardly, things seem well but, one is inwardly discontent. Then help seems to appear from above (high rank in China was marked by red robes and bands). But problems remain. Compromise and spiritual effort may be necessary to settle differences and make adequate preparations. Without patience there will be trouble.

Six in the third place: oppressed himself with stone,
He rests on thorns and pointed plants.
Even at home he cannot see his wife.

A hard worker may benefit, but the time is one of difficulty. Insensitivity leads straight into a brick wall. Alternatively, if there are no difficulties, one invents them. Insubstantial things are now hazardous to him. Recognize the soft, peaceful way as the source of joy and inspiration or shame will continue to intensify.

Nine in the fourth place: oppressed in a glittering carriage, in slow pageant.

Humiliation, but better in the end.
Progress, but probably bringing more difficulty. A certain kind of material 'success' stresses the bonds of companionship with wealthy or powerful people. One need not compromise one's humanitarian principles to please such people.

> *Nine in the fifth place: oppressed by the figure with scarlet trappings,*
> *His nose and feet are cut off.*
> *Accepting this, joy comes slowly.*
> *Benefit in sacrifice.*

There is oppression from above and below. One finds no help from authority, but if one maintains composure, relief will follow, gradually.

> *Six at the top: oppressed by climbing plants, he tells himself,*
> *'If I move I will regret it.'*
> *If he recants and advances, it is auspicious.*

The over-caution of one too long oppressed is shown here. The problems are more imaginary than real, or have been declining for some time. Resolute actions will show that the situation can now be mastered.

☵ 48. CHING (*tzhing*)/The Well

A well is symbolized by water (K'an, above), into which a bucket (Sun, wood) is dipped. The idea of nourishment is added by the image of a plant (Sun) which draws moisture upwards. Ching implies the most fundamental facets of any society — depth and consistency. Depth suggests that stability is built on sensitivity to the most profound needs of man. Consistency implies dependability — a useful well must be a constant, dependable source of water, just as a social structure must be depended on for fairness and opportunity.

The Judgement

The Well. The city may be moved, but not the well.
It neither floods, nor is exhausted.
People come and go to draw from its depths.
If the rope cannot reach the water,
Or the pitcher should break, then misfortune.

Cities in China were relocated as dynasties changed, but the wells remained where they had always been. Thus man's needs remain constant, despite outward circumstances. Human nature does not increase or decrease. The image of the well may symbolize a foundation or some source of benefit. Beware of insufficient depth (superficial understanding or planning) and of carelessness, excess or neglect.

The Image

Water on wood, symbolizing the Well.
The superior man inspires good work from the people,
Encouraging their benevolence toward the community.

The wise person draws water (or uses his efforts) for the good of all. Flexibility and unselfish appreciation of human nature are needed to benefit others. The image of good work, symbolized by the well, reminds us that a muddy well is useless and needs work to reline its sides. Poor relationships and businesses must be repaired.

The Lines

Six at the bottom: one does not drink from a muddy well.
No animals gather at an old well.

Difficulties — perhaps a stale situation can be improved by a change. The image implies that one is wasting oneself. Depleting unappreciated virtues or benevolence leads to heartache.

Nine in the second place: fish may be caught in the ruined well.
The bucket is broken and leaking.

Tension and imminent troubles are indicated. The image shows a well with good water, but only used for fishing. One's container cannot hold fish. Others are not bothered and this may lead to cynicism and one's gradual deterioration. Nothing great can be accomplished, but no specific bad fortune is shown.

Nine in the third place: the well is cleaned, but not used.
Sorrow, for it should be used.
If the king had insight, he would ensure that all benefited.

One is like the disused well: one's abilities are unrecognized, to the sorrow of oneself and to the loss of others. A 'senior' should learn of it. Conditions are unlikely to improve. One should wait.

Six in the fourth place: the well is rebuilt. No mistakes.

Put schemes for inward improvement into operation. Like the rebuilding of a well, this may cause confusion (because the well cannot, meanwhile, be used), but the results will justify it.

Nine in the fifth place: the well is fed by a cool spring.
The man may drink from it.

Profit, promotion and success is indicated. a person is suggested who, like the well, has a desirable quality — spiritual, mental, or material. But the water is not being drawn; the potential is not yet fulfilled.

Six at the top: nothing bars the well.
One can always draw from it.
It is dependable. Supremely auspicious.

One possesses the quality or quantity necessary for success. One whose openness and charity benefits those around and, in turn, himself, is symbolized.

▤ 49. KO (g'r)/Revolution

Changes arising from conflict and conflicts arising from change are at the centre of this hexagram's theme.

The lake (Tui) above fire (Li) shows two elements whose forces are in constant conflict. The lines give advice on how to settle such emnity. Also, Tui and Li represent the daughters but here the younger has usurped her position. Hence the specific idea of revolution. Ko deals with adaptation to it.

The Judgement

Revolution. When the hour strikes, he will be believed.
Great success. Continuing on the path is beneficial.
Guilt vanishes.

However unsatisfactory present conditions, one must wait for the right time to make changes. One will be successful, provided the changes are not selfish.

The Image

Fire within the lake, symbolizing Revolution.
The superior man arranges a calendar,
Marking the order of the seasons.

The seasons, like fire and water, destroy each other as they advance. One who understands change notes the signs and is able to foresee the forthcoming demands of the times beneath symptoms. Thus did prosperous farmers plant. Thus were great battles won.

The Lines

Nine at the bottom: bound in yellow cow hide.

Yellow (the Golden Mean) represents the middle, correct way and the cow means docility. Work hard, without overt ambition. Any attempt to capitalize on current trends would be unfortunate.

> *Six in the second place: when one's hour strikes, one may create a revolution.*
> *Action is auspicious. No mistakes in this.*

A time of good luck and recognition. Changes must be thoroughly prepared and values should be adjusted. The influence of a guiding force may be appropriate now and the results of change must be thought out.

> *Nine in the third place: advance is ominous.*
> *When the people have discussed the plans of revolution three times, then he is trusted.*
> *Waiting is dangerous.*

Excess is disastrous now, particularly excessive conservatism or excessive haste. One can easily be misled by empty contents and ill-founded complaints. Examine every situation thoroughly. Do not be led astray. Discuss and participate with those you trust.

> *Nine in the fourth place: guilt disappears.*
> *The people believe him.*
> *Changing the structure of institutions is auspicious.*

The emphasis here is on unselfish motives and broad, mature views. It is also a warning against pettiness and narrow or superficial thinking. The image of institutions, which professes that certain values be changed, and stresses justice as opposed to hypocrisy. Good luck, promotion and success are indicated for those with humble positions or quiet life-styles.

> *Nine in the fifth place: transforming himself boldly, like a tiger.*
> *He is trusted, even before the oracle is consulted.*

Fortune favours the bold. Change now must be wrought in a decisive manner, with principles 'up front' for all to see — just as a tiger's stripes are visible from afar, when it leaves the long grass and comes into the open.

*Six at the top: the superior man changes subtly, like a
    panther.*
The inferior change their faces.
Advance brings misfortune.
Persevering on the way is auspicious.

Large disturbances have died down and large changes have
been made. Only small changes, as when the panther
moults, are now advisable. Quiet, weak or insignificant
people need only adopt the right expression and their lives
remain uninfluenced. for the revolutionary leader, this is a
fact of life to be accepted. For the quiet person, this is a
means of survival. Be satisfied and obey the rules.

☰ 50. TING (*ding*)/The Cauldron

This hexagram represents nourishment and transformation,
with its emphasis on material matters ordered or
subordinated to abstract considerations. Below, Sun (wood,
wind) fuels Li (flame), suggesting a fire and thus cooking.
The shape of the hexagram was also thought to represent a
cauldron. Ting can auger well for established stable
conditions, since the Chinese cooking pot had three legs
(three being considered the ideal of purity and stability). In
human affairs it symbolizes the executive, judiciary and
legislature. There are also many other parallels — father,
mother, child; husband, wife, mistress etc.

The Judgement

The Ting. Great good fortune.
Success.

The idea of nourishment is enlarged by the hexagram's
attribute suggesting spiritual or abstract values. Thus the
emphasis of Ting is on practical values dedicated to higher
principles.

The Image

Fire over wood symbolizes Ting.
Thus the superior man ensures his fate.
Through his proper position.

Wood (mundane, earthly) nourishes fire. In society, fire symbolizes the moral and cultural superstructure and, in men, spiritual consciousness. The earthly should be ordered according to the nature of the spiritual. Thus the wise person, understanding that it is fate which motivates the unique power in his life, orders his life realistically, according to his understanding of fate. By harmonizing these forces, he enjoys good fortune and progresses spiritually.

The Lines

Six at the bottom: the ting *overturned, in order to clean it.*
The concubine who gives birth to a son is taken to the wife.
  No mistakes.

Here is the image of the overturned *ting*, the 'mistress'. Their position appears humble at first, though they have innate worth. The images of cleansing and fruitfulness suggest that one who is virtuous and talented can succeed, even if in a lowly position at present. Success after sadness is indicated, possibly with another's help.

Nine in the second place: the ting *is full of food.*
My peers are jealous, but cannot harm me. Auspicious.

One is confident of worthwhile undertakings, and secure prosperity (inward, or external).

Nine in the third place: the handles of the ting, *deformed.*
His activity is obstructed.
The pheasant remains uneaten.
The gentle rain brings relief from guilt. Auspicious in the
  end.

If the handles are deformed, the *ting* cannot be lifted, thus food will remain inaccessible. Resources are being wasted.

But if one meets difficulties with virtue, they will be resolved. Obstacles, perhaps loss, followed by happiness.

> *Nine in the fourth place: the legs of a* ting *break, the noble's food is spilled upon the noble.*
> *Misfortune: blame.*

Character, resources or helpers are insufficient. This means failure and, as it is one's own fault, blame. Bad luck, with little success.

> *Six in the fifth place: the* ting *has yellow handles — golden rings.*
> *Keep to the path.*

A time of success and advance. Yellow and gold, indicates modest virtue — someone who is shy, perhaps over-shy. But his virtue attracts those he would not approach. This is the key to his success.

> *Nine at the top: the* ting *has jade rings. Greatly auspicious: Success in everything.*

Jade is lustrous and hard. Strength and benevolence are indicated. The time is one of achievement and recognition. If withdrawal (temporary or permanent) seems suitable, now is a good time.

☳☳ 51. CHEN *(kh'n)*/The Arousing (Thunder-clap)

Both trigrams are Chen, the arousing, which can indicate a time favourable for a second chance. The qualities represented by Chen may be a stimulating force or one which terrifies and disorientates. The emphasis in the advice of Chen is on moderation and skilful, restrained action or reaction.

The Judgement

> *The Thunder-clap brings success.*

Arousal — Ho!
Good cheer — Ha, ha!
Even if all are terrified within one hundred miles,
The worshipper does not drop the sacred implements.

Once one understands the deep shock suggested by Chen, one is immune to its terrors. At a time of unforeseen, disastrous events, this composure ensures that we may perform the most important, delicate duties, and accept even catastrophe with a harmonious and effective spirit.

The Image

Thunder upon thunder symbolizes the Arousing.
Thus the superior man with fearful apprehension
Sets his house in order
And examines his faults.

One can be overtaken by disaster and collapse, but for the wise it gives the inspiration to search his heart to discover strengths and weaknesses, and to arrange his affairs correctly.

The Lines

Nine at the bottom: the Thunder-clap — Ho! Good cheer —
  Ha ha!
Auspicious.

A time when good fortune follows threat, and sudden events indicate a change in one's fortunes.

Six in the second place: the thunder-clap brings danger.
He loses his possessions countless times and must climb the
  nine hills, with no searching.
After seven days, they are returned.

Troubles and loss. If troubles make one lose touch with oneself, things will be made worse. One must be inscrutable. Understand that this loss is, in a sense, inevitable. One may be deprived now, but one's needs will be fulfilled if one is firm within.

Six in the third place: the thunder-clap racks him.
If this stimulates pressing on one's way, no mistakes.

The shock of danger, which seems to penetrate one's insides, can be paralysing. This would be disastrous. One must respond actively to events, in a manner dictated by inner truth and native wit. Difficulties must act as a spur.

Nine in the fourth place: the thunder-clap is dull.

Thick, clouded reactions and a dull mind now will prevent effective response to trouble. In this case, the repercussions are bound to last a long time. A hard lesson, perhaps.

Six in the fifth place: thunder rolling back and forth brings
  danger.
No losses, but matters must be attended to.

Repeated troubles may toss one hither and thither. It is important to keep a clear head and organize one's affairs thoroughly and with insight.

Six at the top: the thunder-clap brings ruin and screaming.
Acting is ominous.
If it strikes one's neighbour but not oneself, no blame — but
  there will be slander from this.

Disaster nearby can destroy effectiveness. One should withdraw, despite angry reactions. Caution may promote good luck, but misfortune is nevertheless in the air.

52. KEN (g'n)/Keeping Still

The trigram Ken (the mountain or keeping still) is doubled here, implying a complete end to movement. Also, in both trigrams, the yang lines have moved as far as they can. Thus there is stillness. This hexagram has strong implications for the achievements of inner peace, and deals with ways in which this can be achieved. Meditation is particularly implied, because in its early stages the difficulties of achieving the quiet mind necessary to further development are obvious to everyone. This hexagram was the lodestone of the Buddhist-inspired, meditative Hsing-I school of Chinese bare-hand fighting.

The Judgement

Keeping still. Keeping the back still,
One can no longer feel one's body.
When one walks in the courtyard,
The people are invisible. No mistake.

Implied is one without inner stillness, who is caught up in others' anxieties and views. The still back is a symbol of deep, inner calm. When no activity disturbs the spinal column, the restless mind gradually quietens. Then one can begin to understand the value and the illusion behind social custom and one's nature. This is the basis of real wisdom.

The Image

Mountain and mountain: Keeping Still.
Thus the thoughts of the superior man
Do not stray beyond his position.

The hardest aspect of meditation is concentration. Not the mental strait-jacket which a child applies to contain his mind within a disliked subject, nor the rapt attention of a man about his hobby, but a superior, flexible quality, which allows the restless heart to produce thoughts, but remain uninvolved in them. This flexible stillness is central to the 'martial arts experience', revered in the Orient. It manifests itself as composure and stillness in the face of approaching danger, broken only by an appropriate and swift response to an enemy's action, at precisely the right moment. Thus, in life, stillness is not negation, but the most effective preparation for any demanding activity. It is a time of planning, in one's own way, and of preparing gradually for later action.

The Lines

Six at the bottom: he keeps his toes still.
If one perseveres, there are no mistakes in this.
The image seems contradictory — the toes (and thus the whole) do not move, though the advice is persistence. The answer is that the initial instinct to proceed is correct, but any doubts should cause one to pause or change one's direction. If you are still, however, stay still.

Six in the second place: he keeps his calves still, but cannot restrain the leader. Frustration.
One cannot communicate to others their folly. If one follows another on the wrong path (a master, for instance) and the legs are reluctant to move, one must leave the other to his fate or fall oneself. A time of worry.

Nine in the third place: he keeps his hips still, and back rigid.
His heart is painful.
This implies artificial rigidity or arrogance. Forceful attitudes will lead to danger. One should try to capture true peace, rather than imposing repressive discipline. The image shows a meditator whose enforced rigidity only irritates and frustrates him. Both success and difficulty are suggested.

Six in the fourth place: his torso is still. No mistakes here.
There is no advantage in forcefulness now. One's heart is still restless. Perfect harmony is a long way off. However, the still torso symbolizes a praiseworthy achievement — a significant step on the way.

Six in the fifth place: he keeps his jaw still.
His speech is orderly.
Guilt vanishes.

Lighthearted, foolish chatter about problems can sometimes make them worse.* It shows deep anxiety behind the façade. One should control one's manner. This is a time of advance and harmony.

Nine at the top: keeping still with honourable virtue.
Auspicious.
Benevolent, calm acceptance, which accumulates virtue. A time of harmony, tranquillity and good luck.

☶ 53. CHIEN (*jee'n*) /Development (Procession)

This hexagram implies progress, in a measured, orderly way. Above is Sun, the eldest daughter; below, Ken, the youngest son. Both grow and progress step by step, in the same way as a tree (Sun) on the mountain (Ken). There it must weave its roots into the thin soil to ensure stability in its exposed position.

The Judgement

Development. Marriage of a maiden.
Auspicious.
Perseverance is beneficial.
The Judgement indicates the significance of social mores, custom, tradition, and an individual's integration within the community through subjugating personal inclinations. The formalities leading to marriage were unhurried and could not be rushed by outside forces. Correct and gradual development of the relationship was considered the prime

---

* Confucius expands on this theme as follows: 'If language is not correct, then what is said is not what is meant. then what ought to be done is not done and, if things remain undone, morals and arts will deteriorate. Then justice will go awry. If this occurs, the people will be lost in helpless confusion. Thus what is said matters above all and there must be no carelessness in this.'

requisite for successful union.

The Image

A tree upon the mountain symbolizes Development.
Thus the superior man, maintaining his virtue,
Improves the customs of society.

The tree on the mountain grows slowly, only gradually becoming a visible landmark for the people. Personality must develop through patient perseverance. Custom must be observed and influence must increase in gentle stages. Chien is favourable for affairs developing step by step.

The Lines

Six at the bottom: gradually, the wild geese approach the shore.
The boy meets danger.
There is talk, but no blame here.

The most constructive attribute, marriage, is stressed throughout the lines by the symbol of the wild goose, which represented perfect fidelity (in the broadest sense) as it was thought to take only one mate during its lifetime. The line shows one setting out on a demanding journey. He makes mistakes, but this will be good for him.

Six in the second place: gradually, the wild geese approach the boulders.
They may eat and drink contentedly. Good fortune.

One reaches rest and safety. The way ahead is visible. The ideagrams emphasize that one's fortune should be shared, or put to unselfish use.

Nine in the third place: gradually, the wild geese approach the high wilderness.
The explorer sets forth: he will not return.
The woman is with child but will not deliver it.
Misfortune. Defend yourself against robbers.

One has gone too far, too high, and is in a hostile place. Arrogance, thoughtlessness, or selfish individualism bring trouble. Persevere without using force or aggressive actions. A time of disharmony and loss is indicated.

Six in the fourth place: gradually, the wild geese approach the tree, seeking a flat perch.
No mistake here.

One is in an awkward position, through no apparent fault of one's own. The geese will find a resting place and be content, but trees are not suitable for the web-footed birds, so danger is indicated. Humility will help to avoid it, until it is time to move on.

Nine in the fifth place: gradually, the wild geese approach the peaks.
For three years the woman is fertile, then nothing can prevent her.
Auspicious.

One moving rapidly towards the heights can easily leave others behind and then suffer from bitterness. But this is a passing phase and harmony will return, helped by internal or external adjustment.

Nine at the top: gradually, the wild geese approach the farthest heights.
Their feathers, fluttering down, will be used in decoration.
Good fortune.

The image of a flight of wild geese winging toward heaven was symbolic of virtuous, auspicious endeavour and any feathers collected were used in religious adornments. The achievements indicated include leaving the past behind. One's virtue is recognized, and a new life awaits.

≣ 54. KUEI MEI (*guay may*) /The Marrying Maiden

Above is Chen (thunder, the arousing, the eldest son);

below is Tui (youngest daughter, lake, the joyous). Thus a young girl is represented, following an older man, with joy on her side and the quality of arousing on his. The central metaphor of the marrying maiden is highly specialized. Custom allowed a sort of 'junior wife' who was welcomed into the family to care for the husband's most intimate needs. The moral admonitions which result from this metaphor concern the subtle, delicate conditions which must be fulfilled in relationships. In purely divinatory interpretation, the situations portrayed emphasize impermanence, because the status of the surrogate wife was not sanctified by social decree.

The Judgement

The Marrying Maiden. Undertakings are ominous.
No benefit anywhere.

Enormous tact and reserve was necessary so that the young 'mistress' would not usurp the influence of the generally more mature woman who fulfilled the demanding formal duties of a wife. In modern relationships success depends on reserve and compromise as the essential expression of affection. The mundane meaning is that one is involved with others because of one's usefulness — the result of an unspoken, perhaps hypocritical need of others.

The Image

Thunder over the lake, symbolizing the Marrying Maiden.
Thus the superior man understands the short-lived
And matches his virtue to the demands of the eternal.

The thunder-storm stirs the lake, creating bright waves. Thus, there is attraction: it is bright and glittering, but has no permanence. Once one understands that one's position is somewhat artificial one will only try to be what one is expected to be. Obviously, this hexagram does not bode well for marriage or permanent undertakings. One should be austere in behaviour and expectation.

The Lines

Nine at the bottom: the marrying maiden is a mistress.
The lame man can walk. Advance is auspicious.
A time of achievement — even with limited resources. An inferior position is indicated. If one accepts the position, one has a definite sphere of action within which to accomplish goals.

Nine in the second place: the one-eyed can see.
Perseverance is beneficial to the solitary.
A time of no advance, but one should be secure. The image represents a disappointed girl.

Six in the third place: the marrying maiden is enslaved.
She can be accepted as no more than this.
If secure, one may lose: if insecure, one may succeed — but wait for the right time. One achieves one's aim, but finds the accompanying duties onerous or unfulfilling. One has been unrealistic in self-assessment and must accept a position which is lowly or uncertain.

Nine in the fourth place: the marrying maiden appears undecided.
Sooner or later, she will marry.
One is weighing the future against one's instincts. A time for changing one's course or waiting. If holding oneself in reserve through self-esteem, good opportunity may appear to have been lost — but one will find the appropriate opportunity.

Six in the fifth place: the emperor gives his daughter in common marriage.
Her dress not yet so ornate as that of the bridesmaids.
The moon is almost full. Good fortune.
The line indicates one of superior virtue who accepts a lowly position without bitterness. Good fortune in the

limited circumstances, or perhaps in future progress. Fulfilment and success are indicated.

Six at the top: the maiden's basket is empty.
The man's knife draws no blood from the sheep. No benefit.
The symbolism of an empty ritual suggests an irreverent, uncommitted attitude. Alternatively, one is unable to fill the role demanded. Apparent success is unmatched by real rewards.

☰☷ 55. FENG (*f'ng*)/Greatness (Fullness)

Chen (thunder, arousing) is above and Li (flame, clinging) is below. Together they suggest a clear, brilliant spirit within movement and thus the idea of brilliant success. Other attributes of the trigram emphasize abundance and brilliance, which can only be short-lived (for instance, the attribute of flame clinging to woods symbolizes a raging forest fire). A time to enjoy what one has without expectations.

The Judgement

Greatness. Success.
The king attains greatness. No sadness now.
It is like the sun at midday.
The midday sun will shortly begin to fall. Additionally, its warming, benevolent effect on the world suggests unselfishness and benevolence toward all and this attitude forestalls arrogance and temper when good fortune has passed.

The Image

Thunder and lightning playing together, symbolizing
Greatness.

Thus the superior man judges disputes
And effects punishments.

The energetic clarity suggested by Chen and Li, respectively, shows both how abundance can be created by applying energy and insight, and how one may secure one's prosperity and avoid excesses once this has been achieved. The wise person avoids complacency and is temperate and judicious in handling his affairs.

The Lines

Nine at the bottom: he meets his spiritual leader.
They associate for ten days, without mistakes.
Advance brings improvement.

This is a time when others' aid may bring reward. Here, two parties with complementary qualities (represented by the attributes of the trigrams) are symbolized. They may come in contact naturally, or with some effort. The result will be a fruitful association during a full cycle of time.

Six in the second place: the screen is so great, that stars can
be seen at midday.
Advancing with energy brings suspicion and hate.
Advancing with truth brings good fortune.

A barrier before the sun, here symbolizes an intrigue which blocks one's success effectively — the sun is so effectively blocked that all light disappears. Actively countering this situation would bring only misfortune, so one must either establish a good relationship with the others concerned, or pursue one's course modestly and correctly. Loss or difficulty followed by good fortune is indicated.

Nine in the third place: bamboo so thick that stars can be
seen at midday.
His right arm is disabled. No blame.

Here success is eclipsed by a fast-processing element which takes the situation completely out of one's hands. A time of loss and difficulty.

Nine in the fourth place: the curtain is so thick that stars can be seen at midday.

He meets his spiritual leader. Auspicious.

The eclipsing influence is on the wane, and one is able to make contact with a party whose qualities complement one's own (see line one). Unsettled, unharmonious conditions are indicated. Opportunities may present themselves.

Six in the fifth place: he attracts brilliant men, who bring prosperity and fame. Auspicious.

One's own good qualities will attract others who are able. Perhaps others' abilities are now revealed for the first time. A time of help, promotion and recognition.

Six at the top: his family are enclosed within the great house.

Watching the gate, no-one is seen. Misfortune.

One who strives for splendour, but become arrogant, is indicated. The result is worry, loss or selfish illusions. A time of conflict and difficulty for all but the humble.

☲☶ 56. LU (*liu*)/The Stranger

Li (fire) above Ken (the mountain) symbolizes a fire on the mountain. Without abundant foliage to fuel it, it will be short-lived. The two principles — one keeping still, the other moving and energetic — are strangers to each other, and the restless, searching nature of fire adds the implication of wandering. The person indicated by Lu is one of life's travellers. The travels may be internal or actual, but are prompted by a real, inner motive.

The Judgement

The Stranger. Success in small things.
Auspicious, if one perseveres on this path.

The traveller will never achieve permanent influence.

Therefore, one must be flexible, sincere and undemanding so as not to take out of things more than one puts in. The wanderer must be reserved in his behaviour for he is vulnerable to grasping or demanding people. Others are, similarly, vulnerable to him, because they are conditioned by the illusions of secure circumstances.

The Image

Fire burns on the mountain, symbolizing the Traveller.
Thus the superior man acts with caution and insight,
When effecting punishments.
He has no time for litigation.

The mountain fire is a temporary phenomenon, symbolizing a man who does not become involved with attitudes and events which would complicate his life or delay his travels. On the whole, Lu is unfavourable for permanent or binding agreement or enterprises.

The Lines

Six at the bottom: a traveller engrossed with pretty things
invites misfortune.

One who is in a vulnerable position should not become involved with trivial or inferior conditions. If forced into this position, he should maintain caution. Similarly, one should respect others' attitudes. One may find oneself at odds with surrounding circumstances.

Six in the second place: the traveller arrives at the inn, and
he is a man of substance.
He gains the loyalty of a young servant.

A time of advance and success, possibly through travel. The traveller's wealth symbolizes the ability to be in touch with one's innermost being, which produces harmonious behaviour and attracts others.

Nine in the third place: the traveller burns down the inn.
He is deserted by his servants.
One's own way brings danger.

Trouble within one's immediate environment is indicated here. One is shown involved in matters outside one's area of competence. Perhaps one is meddling but 'inner communication' has certainly been lost. Others are unsympathetic towards the traveller.

Nine in the fourth place: the traveller finds a quiet shelter.
He has all he needs, but his heart is uneasy.

A time of success, possibly involving travel. The image shows one who has ceased wandering and has found a secure niche. Perhaps he is a person who knows how to limit his behaviour and needs to his situation. The situation may be insecure and loss likely. If one is by nature a traveller, one will feel restricted and uncomfortable in the situation.

Six in the fifth place: the traveller shoots a pheasant with a
* single arrow.*
Thus, honour and responsibility.

A time of success, promotion and reward is indicated. Here, a traveller is skilful and observes the correct formalities and thus wins acceptance. Accept the forms of your situation, however foreign they may appear.

Nine at the top: a bird's nest on fire.
The traveller laughs, then sorrows.
He loses his cow through carelessness. Ominous.

One who is reckless or incautious and loses or destroys something valuable or essential to one's security is indicated here. Arrogance or selfish cynicism is shown as an accompaniment. In his unrelentingly selfish actions, he loses his flexibility and modesty.

☴ 57. SUN (*sune*)/The Penetrating Wind (the Gentle)

Both trigrams are Sun — the wind, the gentle or penetrating quality. To these attributes is added the idea of harmony. Sun also symbolizes wood or plants. Plants bend with the wind, here giving the idea of flexible, harmonious activity. The condition implied by Sun brings quiet, relaxed, subtle attitudes and actions. It helps develop a harmonious, non-wilful attitude toward conditions, things and people. Sun augers well for new undertakings, particularly those which involve movement.

The Judgement

> *The Penetrating Wind. Success in small ways.*
> *Benefit in advance.*
> *Benefit in seeing the great man.*

The influence of the Gentle is one which establishes enduring conditions by modest, gradual effort. Often this requires the help of a stronger or more influential person. A time of influencing more by strength of character than by direct action. This carries the danger of becoming over-involved.

The Image

> *Wind blowing after wind symbolizes the Gentle.*
> *Thus the superior man broadcasts his commands*
> *And secures his affairs.*

Here a definite goal is indicated, together with care in undertaking its execution. The wise person prepares the way for what is to follow, widening his influence by suggestion and leadership.

The Lines

> *Six at the bottom: blowing to and fro, persevering like a*

warrior is beneficial.
Unsettled conditions are indicated: one might succeed and lose. If a path ahead is seen, one should advance: if one has doubts, one must hold back or withdraw. Firmness is the correct way.

Nine in the second place: the wind beneath a bed.
He summons witches and exorcists.
Auspicious: no blame in this.
Subtle, dark forces seem to undermine one's plans and they must be traced back to their source and brought out into the open. Openness and honesty succeed. Auspicious for communication and academic pursuits.

Nine in the third place: gusting wind, repeated. Regret.
A time of unexpected advance or difficulty is indicated. The image suggests undue pondering until it is obvious that one is incapable of making a decision. This would bring embarrassment and demean one in the eyes of others.

Six in the fourth place: guilt disappears.
The hunter traps game for the three purposes.
The three purposes were: sacrifice, honouring guests and everyday meals. Thus, one in a responsible position is pictured making full use of his resources and considering all factors (either practical, emotional and moral) in a balanced fashion. Thus one can find good in everything. A time of success and good luck.

Nine in the fifth place: benefit through persevering. Guilt
   disappears.
Benefit in every way.
Not in the beginning, but in the end.
Before the change, three days.
After the change, three days. Auspicious.
The image shows an imperfect situation. This may not be obvious. Careful reform is needed and one should not throw the baby out along with the bath-water. Afterwards,

one must be prepared to continue changes until things are right. This will inevitably bring success.

Nine at the top: the wind beneath a bed.
He loses his wealth, and his weapons.
In one's own way, misfortune.

The quiet, penetrating power of Sun has reached its limit. There may be success, but loss and difficulties are likely. One has lost' one's ability to deal with evil. If one then penetrates deeply into a situation and finds bad conditions, one is helpless. Then immediate withdrawal would be the only course.

䷹ 58. TUI (*dweah*)/Joyousness

The trigram Tui, (lake, youngest daughter, the joyous) doubled, forms this hexagram. The happiness of the youngest daughter shows in traditional, cheerful singing as she goes about her business. Tui also represents success, and prosperity. It is thus favourable for business projects and new undertakings. But, for existing relationships and undertakings there may be misfortune and quarrels.

The Judgement

Joyousness. Success.
Keeping to one's way is favourable.

Uncomplicated, infectious joy is indicated. If joyousness is underlined by steadfastness, it will influence the hardest heart. Joy without and perseverance within is the ideal balance of qualities now.

The Image

The lake replenishing the lake symbolizes Joyousness.
Thus the superior man studies and practises
With his companions.

The two lakes joined symbolize the reinforcing effect of happiness, knowledge and wisdom shared between men. The Image also indicates the need to measure one's joy against objective standards. Within relationships, pleasure can easily be a selfish feeling, unrelated to the state of the other party. However, pleasure shared is doubled.

The Lines

Nine at the bottom: inner joyousness. Auspicious.
A secure, self-contained contentment is shown, bringing its possessor freedom from desire and compulsion. A time of harmony — but the danger of complacency, even selfishness, and thus conflict, is indicated.

Nine in the second place: sincere joyousness brings good fortune.
Guilt vanishes.
A time of harmony and advance. One should not become involved in low pleasures which might be embarrassing to oneself or others, now or later.

Six in the third place: indulging joyousness. Ominous.
One with only a spiritual vacuum within, and the appreciation of joy without, will be tempted into worthless, unfulfilling pleasures. Inevitably, one will lose touch with oneself more and more. A time when one may be deceived and thus make dangerous mistakes.

Nine in the fourth place: calculated joyousness is not a peace.
With cautious correctness, good fortune.
A time of material advance is indicated, if one is cautious. The image advises one to enjoy all pleasures without compulsion or greed.

Nine in the fifth place: confidence in the declining is dangerous.
However sincere one is, one can become involved with

unworthy circumstances or people. Only by recognizing this tendency can one avoid danger.

Six at the top: seduced by joyousness.
A time of pleasant or helpful circumstances, but no real success. One who loses touch with his deeper nature and sense of direction is now swept along by fate and circumstance.

59. HUAN (*hw'n*) /Dispersion

Wind (Sun) above the water (K'an) indicates the dispersion of water — the spume blown from the waves by the gusting wind. A wasteful dissolution of energies is the most obvious image here, but Huan indicates also how energy stored or blocked up can be released by gentleness.

The Judgement

Dispersion. Success.
The king approaches the temple.
Crossing the great water is of benefit.
Persevering benefits.
The emphasis here is on the dissolution of divisiveness by the sharing of common, higher activities, such as religious ritual. The king, here, symbolizes the person of great personal quality or authority, who is necessary to unite men divided by egoism. The upper trigram also means wood, suggesting boats on the water. This, together with the advice 'to cross the great water', suggests benefits through travel.

The Image

Wind blowing on the water, symbolizing Dispersion.
Thus the ancient rulers, piously, sacrificed to the Absolute,

And erected temples for their successors.

Whilst the Judgement suggests men whose hardness is broken down by receiving a charitable impulse, here the giver of charity is emphasized, uniting others in common piety. The idea of continuity is suggested by the temple-building image.

The Lines

Six at the bottom: rescue with the aid of a good horse.
Auspicious.

Vigorous and selfless action is stressed here and this may be necessary to prevent quarrelling and misunderstanding. A time of advance.

Nine in the second place: dispersion spurs him on towards shelter.
Guilt vanishes now.

The image shows one who, realizing that divisiveness and bad feeling are on the increase takes steps to establish firm, reliable conditions. These may be within himself, or external. A time of mixed fortune.

Six in the third place: he disperses his egoism. No guilt here.

Renouncing the self can be useful — for instance, when one has difficult or stressful circumstances to deal with. But it may make one neglect oneself.

Six in the fourth place: he disperses cliques. Supremely auspicious.
Dispersion is followed by accumulation, though ordinary men are unaware of this.

A time of mixed fortune: advance and success are likely; loss is possible. By ignoring personal commitments or private friendships in favour of wider considerations, one is able to be objective and decisive. An unusually wise overview is required for this.

Nine in the fifth place: pronouncements like sweat

dispersing.
Dispersion from the king's palace.
No mistakes in this.

During disorganized times, when energies and resources are scattered, a crisis point (like the time of sweating during severe illness) is the time when all can be made cohesive through one authoritative, visionary ideal. But great energy and generosity are needed to capitalize on this rallying point. A time of good fortune and promotion.

Nine at the top: dispersing the way of blood; avoiding;
*   going.*
No mistake in this.

One is pictured approaching a dangerous and potentially wounding situation. One should consider consequences. A time of relief from unpleasant or dangerous circumstances, or a change for the better is indicated.

≡≡ 60. CHIEH (*jhee-eh*) /Limitation

K'an (water, danger) above Tui (the lake, joyous) suggests a lake which will overflow unless restrained. Striving towards ideals and hoping for perfection are not in themselves unrealistic, but without the awareness of limitation and without restraint in personal behaviour, they are hopeless dreams.

The Judgement

Limitations. Success.
Do not persevere in bitter limitation.

Limitations, restraint and thrift are sterling qualities, which can lighten impoverishment and increase one's resources. But if limitation is inimical to people, or to the basic functioning of their circumstances, it is frustrating and destructive. Thus one should keep a sense of proportion.

The Image

Water above the lake symbolizes Limitations.
The superior man quantifies, regulates,
And measures the nature of conduct and virtue.

The lake has limits, but water is without limits — thus it must be contained. Only determining one's talents and weaknesses, and the limitations of the way ahead, can one follow a particular path and avoid being pulled hither and thither by temporary circumstances. Nevertheless, one should not stifle potential.

The Lines

Nine at the bottom: he does not go out beyond door and courtyard.
No mistakes in this.

A time when advance is unfavourable. Waiting and discreet preparation will clear the way for advance when the time comes.

Nine in the second place: he does not go out beyond gate and courtyard.
Misfortune.

When the time for action arrives, one must take it. Hesitation at this time will mean opportunities irrevocably lost, or even disaster.

Six in the third place: he is without restraint.
He will have cause to sorrow. No blame.

A time when any extravagance will meet with harsh consequences. The person illustrated is prone to excess: he may be a hedonist, or tend to severity of arrogance. The fault lies in oneself: this is the meaning of free will.

Six in the fourth place: contented restraint. Success.

Restraint must be natural: this feeling cannot be achieved if one's limitations (whether imposed by oneself, or by one's situation) are either too strict or too lenient. A time when the correct conduct symbolized by Chieh brings rewards.

Nine in the fifth place: sweetly restrained, he finds honour in advance. Good fortune.

If one is to get one's way, it is important not to impose limitations on others, which one would not accept oneself (especially if leading others). If one can impose limits on others which fit the situation and which do not restrict their freedom, great achievements are possible.

Six at the top: bitter limitation.
Misfortune if one continues.
Guilt will vanish.

A time when persisting in one's attitudes or actions will bring misfortune. Imposing harsh restrictions on others will meet with resentment, sooner or later. If, however, the conditions demand that limitations be applied, one should first look to correcting oneself, then one can be free of blame or guilt.

☰ 61. CHUNG FU (*jhoong fih*) /Understanding (Truth)

Tui (youngest daughter, the joyous) below Sun (eldest daughter, the gentle) suggests a kindly older sister whose influence causes the younger girl to follow happily. Thus Chung Fu indicates a time of confidence, and sincerity. Through the image of wind (Sun) ruffling the waters of the lake (Tui), the hexagram presents the idea of manifestation of the invisible. The powerful stimulate the weak or inferior by gentleness. The weaker element responds with confidence.

The Judgement

Understanding. Pigs and fishes.
Auspicious.

Benefit in crossing the great water.
Benefit in perseverance.

It is possible to influence even the most stubborn, or difficult people or circumstances — symbolized by the pigs and fishes — through the power of universal truth, to which all things respond. This is not simply through common interest, sympathy, empathy, or some esoteric bond, but through the awareness of the divine spirit which transcends cultural differences or personal values and which is in every thing and every person.

The Image

Wind on the lake symbolizes Truth.
The superior man carefully judges litigation
Thus avoiding executions.

The ancient Chinese justice system was conducted by an examining magistrate. It was considered that penetrating enquiry produced an understanding which would avoid needless punishment. Here, the emphasis is upon penetrating understanding which transcends social, cultural or other differences between people.

The Lines

Nine at the bottom: considering beforehand is beneficial.
Other considerations, outside him, bring anxiety.

A time of success, helped by others, and hard work. The line warns against deviousness and facile or selfish judgements, or unworthy associates.

Nine in the second place: a crane calling amongst the water grass.
Her brood responds.
I have delicious viands: I will share them with you.

A time of good fortune. Clear, unselfish virtue at the core of one's self is the root of all real influence. It spreads as surely as ripples on a pond.

Six in the third place: he meets his friend.
He beats the drum; he stops.
He sobs; he sings.

The image shows one who is deeply dependent on another. No admonition suggesting good or ill is given, but the time indicated is one when conditions fluctuate between good and bad. Gain may follow loss, or vice versa.

Six in the fourth place: the moon is nearly full.
One dray horse escapes: one continues faithfully.
No mistakes here.

When the moon is nearly full, it is near to waning. Thus, realizing how the tides of fortune change, one should be humble and modestly seek the inner meaning in one's situation. The 'horse' image shows one of a pair moving away, breaking up the relationship. The other can do nothing, but continues on his course. Promotion is indicated, and a separation is possible.

Nine in the fifth place: he possesses understanding, which
    embraces all.
No mistakes in this.

A time of harmony and achievement. However, the line symbolizes one who holds a situation together by his clear, undiscriminating empathy with all. If this binding force were withdrawn, disorder and hostility would enter the situation.

Nine at the top: the cock's crow pierces heaven.
Continuing is ominous.

The crowing cock is like one whose effective virtue lies in convincing others of its presence and efficacy. This will eventually prove disastrous. A time of difficulty or complication is indicated for some. Those with modest or humble life-styles may, however, succeed now.

☰☷ 62. HSIAO KUA (*zheeou gw'r*)/Excess of the Small

Chen (thunder, arousing) is above Ken (the mountain, stillness), indicating strength which is trapped by the force above. This idea of strength or virtue contained by weak or inferior elements represents one who is unable to meet the demands of his situation. Meanness or lack of steady purpose is indicated here.

The Judgement

> *Excess of the Small. Success.*
> *Small things may be achieved: great things may not be achieved.*
> *Perseverance is beneficial.*
> *Like the song-bird.*
> *Upward motion is not good;*
> *Remaining low is good.*
> *Greatly auspicious.*

The modesty which stems from recognizing one's limitations is a virtue, but it can be seen as weakness if it is not accompanied by conscientiousness. One should understand the demands of one's situation, and not expect great success. Like the bird whose song presages its descent, we should not strive for great achievements.

The Image

> *Thunder over the mountain, symbolizing Excess of the Small.*
> *The modesty of the superior man is humility;*
> *His mourning is grief,*
> *And his economy is miserly.*

The wise person who, like a man in the mountains, hearing thunder directly above, recognizes the nature of the time.

148

Thus he pays strict attention to the form, the custom, and is extremely humble in his behaviour, tending always to greater humility than is strictly necessary. One can only fall if one climbs.

The Lines

Six at the beginning: the bird soars high. Misfortune.
A time of apparent good fortune, followed by loss is indicated. One should respect the nature of one's position and resources, and not attempt to go beyond these. If one is unprepared to meet responsibilities, misfortune will result.

Six in the second place: she passes her spiritual father, in
*   favour of the spiritual mother.*
He passes the ruler and meets the minister.
No mistakes in this.
The rules are bent or broken. One finds oneself in a position for which one is unprepared. However, the correct course is to carry on conscientiously, putting one's best foot forward.

Nine in the third place: without scrupulous precaution,
*   others may strike him from behind. Ominous.*
One who is over-confident, careless, or simply vulnerable through inadequacy should beware of hidden dangers. Danger is not unavoidable, but great caution is vital.

Nine in the fourth place: he meets things temperately.
No mistakes here.
Danger in advance.
Persevere, with caution.
A time of likely difficulty, though it will probably be temporary. One should be cautious, conciliatory and remain uninvolved.

Six in the fifth place: heavy clouds in the west, but no rain
*   fall.*

The prince shoots one arrow into a cave and hits his prey.
The line indicates one who is somewhat isolated from the position he wishes to achieve. The person who reaches that position — be it oneself or another — will succeed through his real achievements and the aptness of his qualifications. If one is choosing helpers, their genuine worth must be separated from their reputations.

Six at the top: he passes him over, without meeting him.
The song-bird flies away.
Misfortune: destruction.
In a time when details are important, one attends to generalities. If, when small opportunities are seen, one attempts large undertakings and if one has good fortune, and tries to take undue advantage of it, one will meet a bitter end. Only people of hard-working modesty will have good fortune now.

63. CHI CHI (*jhee tzhee*) /Completion

In this hexagram, broken and unbroken lines are distributed equally. The trigram's K'an (above, water) and Li (fire) produce the idea of completion through the image of boiling water. Thus two ideas are present: on the one hand, it is a time of success, harmony and coming to fruition; on the other hand, the balanced nature shown by Chi Chi (like the full moon or the midday sun images used frequently in the I) means influence and success will shortly wane. This unending flux is the basic meaning behind the *I Ching*.

The Judgement

Completion. Success in small things.
Persevering is beneficial.
At first, good fortune.
Later, disorder.

Now is the time when only small matters can be successfully undertaken. Similarly, the success and creative blossoming brought about by this peak of energies is a time to attend to small matters, and one should not allow one's good fortune to prompt careless or relaxed attitudes. One need not suffer unduly if one truly understands that decay must follow fruition.

The Image

> *Water above fire, symbolizing Completion.*
> *Thus the superior man contemplates the nature of misfortune*
> *And prepares himself.*

Water and fire here symbolize a creative tension which produces good results. But the two forces are by their nature hostile, and their harmony is a fragile thing. The Judgement advises that whatever is successful or already established should be carefully tended and maintained, without expansion. What is incomplete should be finished, or brought to fruition without delay.

The Lines

> *Nine at the bottom: braking.*
> *The fox wets his tail. No mistakes.*

The nature of things now seems to be advance, pressing forward, blossoming. If one is not supremely cautious, and if one diverges from one's own principles only a little, there will be unfortunate consequences. However, by following one's principles and acting discriminately — however unpopular or unfashionable this is — one will avoid any real harm. A time of difficulty, when one should not undertake anything, is indicated.

> *Six in the second place: she loses the screen from the carriage window.*

151

Do not seek it. It will be found, after seven days.

A time of difficulty, even loss is indicated, at first. The image refers to the danger of pushing oneself forward and acting immodestly. Do not do so: the right time will come after the present cycle has been fulfilled.

Nine in the third place: the great emperor subdued the barbarian borderlands, and conquered them after three years.

Do not employ the inferior.

A time of difficulty and conflict is indicated but success will come later, with perseverance. One should not be lax or over-confident and there is a danger of romanticizing or identifying with foolish aims. One should examine one's situation and resources carefully.

Six in the fourth place: he has finery, but wears rags.

He is cautious the day long.

A time when caution will maintain the status quo. One may have what one needs, though not extraordinary success. Within a successful situation, hidden dangers may lurk.

Nine in the fifth place: the sacrifice of the neighbour, slaughtering an ox in the west is not so blessed as the small offering of the man to the west.

Ostentatious, or large schemes and circumstances are not favoured at this time. The line specifically advises modesty and simplicity rather than outward shows of virtue or resource. Small affairs are auspicious.

Six at the top: his head is wet. Danger.

The nature of the time is forward movement. If one pauses, or allows oneself to be complacent or self-congratulatory, further danger will immediately accrue. A time of opportunity, but where stable circumstances can conceal bad influence.

64. WEI CHI (*way tzhee*) /Before Completion

Li (flame) above K'an (water) here symbolizes the sun rising from the sea at dawn. Although this is the last hexagram, the lines are not in their correct places. The time indicated is spring and thus, a time of effort and preparation for completion is indicated. This hexagram is favourable for fresh projects — it contains great hope for the future.

The Judgement

Before Completion. Success.
The little fox, nearly over the water,
Wets his tail.
No benefit in this.

The little fox is a classic Chinese folk image. If he does not advance cautiously he can fail or be harmed at the last moment. More broadly, the image suggests a strange or potentially hostile situation. One may have been lucky and avoided harm so far, but only conscious, contemplative attitudes will secure your position. The situation lacks cohesion or a unifying force. Perhaps this can be provided by an ideal or shared ambition.

The Image

Fire over the water symbolizes Before Completion.
Thus the superior man is clear as to the nature of things
And allots an appropriate place to each.

The direction of fire is upward: the direction of water is downward. In the relationship symbolized by Wei Chi, they are irreconcilable. Thus one should make a realistic examination of the nature of one's circumstances.

The Lines

Six at the bottom: he wets his tail. Guilt lies here.

Confused, unsettled conditions produce the temptation to take rapid action. But if the time for advance has not come, one will be humiliated. Refrain until the way is clear. Achievement will be difficult and successes will be limited and unrewarding.

Nine in the second place: he applies the brake.
Persevering is auspicious.
For the time being, one must wait. The way ahead will clear and one should, therefore, gather one's strength and resources and prepare. Then success will come naturally at the correct moment. A time when unusual, or crude attempts to advance will bring trouble.

Six in the third place: before completion, proceeding is ominous.
It is beneficial to cross the great water.
The time for action arrives — but one is inadequate for the undertaking. Continuing would be disastrous. One should withdraw, make a break, and start a new activity.

Nine in the fourth place: persevering is beneficial.
Guilt vanishes.
He must use great force to subdue the barbarian borderlands.
He knows, within three years, he will receive great reward.
The time to act has arrived. It may be dangerous, but it is imperative to act or the opportunity will be lost. A time of success and profit.

Six in the fifth place: persevering is auspicious.
No guilt here.
The brilliance of the superior man is steadfast.
Good fortune.
A time of success, when everything appears better than before. Maintain empathy with others and seek to find order within disorder.

Nine at the top: he celebrates with wine.

No mistakes in this.
If he wets his head, he loses his wits.
The avoidance of danger is emphasized here. At this time, when one has achieved harmony within one's circle, there is an ever-present danger of excess or carelessness. This would undo the good work already accomplished.

APPENDIX

Hexagram Identification Chart

Trigrams Upper ► Lower ▼	Ch'ien ☰	Chen ☳	K'an ☵	Ken ☶	K'un ☷	Sun ☴	Li ☲	Tui ☱
Ch'ien ☰	1	34	5	26	11	9	14	43
Chen ☳	25	51	3	27	24	42	21	17
K'an ☵	6	40	29	4	7	59	64	47
Ken ☶	33	62	39	52	15	53	56	31
K'un ☷	12	16	8	23	2	20	35	45
Sun ☴	44	32	48	18	46	57	50	28
Li ☲	13	55	63	22	36	37	30	49
Tui ☱	10	54	60	41	19	61	38	58

Trigrams and Their Attributes

Symbol	Characteristics	Season
Ch'ien (Heaven)	yang, strong, creative, light-father	late autumn-early winter
K'un (Earth)	yin, devoted, receptive, dark, yielding-mother	late summer-early autumn
Chen (Thunder)	arousing, strong, excited, moving-eldest son	spring
K'an (Water)	deep, dangerous, abysmal, cunning-middle son	winter
Ken (Mountain)	quiet, stubborn, keeping still-youngest son	late winter-early spring
Sun (Wind, Wood)	yielding, penetrating, gentle-eldest; daughter	late spring-early summer
Li (Fire, Lightning, Sun)	clinging, hot, agitated, beautiful-middle daughter	summer
Tui (Lake)	joyous, soft, laughing-youngest daughter	autumn

Also available in the Paths to Inner Power series...

UNDERSTANDING NUMEROLOGY

The power to know anybody

D. JASON COOPER

Hidden in the letters of our names, in the dates of our birth, in the very words we use, there lies a power. Called numerology, it reveals both our inner natures and our future destiny. It was known to the Babylonians, the Greeks, the Phoenicians and the Chaldeans, and now D. Jason Cooper's informative and easy-to-follow introduction will help you to plot a successful course through life today. Discover the meaning of numbers, construct and interpret your personal numeroscope and uncover the meaning of your destiny number.

UNDERSTANDING ASTRAL PROJECTION

Exploration in a world beyond the body

ANTHONY MARTIN

Astral projection is the ability to move beyond the physical body, to explore a world 'out of the body'. Once mastered, the techniques of astral projection can be used at will to escape from the confines of the physical body, move vast distances through space, penetrate apparently solid matter and experience strange encounters on the infinite inner planes. With this book as your guide, you can take your first steps on the strangest journey of your life — a trip beyond the body.

MEDITATION: THE INNER WAY

How to use meditation as a powerful force for self-improvement

NAOMI HUMPHREY

Meditation is a marvellous self-help tool for a wide variety of physical, emotional and psychological problems. *Meditation: The Inner Way* explains the basic techniques used by the many and varied systems of meditation and shows that these techniques can be easily learned and applied to your life today. Using clear instructions, in plain language, and carefully selected exercises, Naomi Humphrey shows how meditation can be used as a powerful force for self-improvement.

HOW TO DEVELOP YOUR ESP

A programme to help you realize your full psychic potential

ZAK MARTIN

How to Develop Your ESP sets out in clear, easy-to-follow terms tried and tested techniques for developing ESP (Extra-Sensory Perception) in its many forms, including telepathy, precognition, dowsing, divination, clairvoyance, psychometry, psychokinesis and dream interpretation. Whether you have ever thought you were 'psychic' or not, Zak Martin's programme will quickly help you develop your natural gifts to the full. '*There is a universe of untapped power, an infinite resource within the psychic reach of every person.*'